We find ourselves in times of unprecedented change on a scale that is both challenging and threatening for the way we think and do church today. The mastery and office of the Christendom theological epistemologies, methodologies, and practices function more and more in a vacuum than at the core and the edges of people's, churches' and communities' lives and worlds. *We Are Here Now: A New Missional Era* is a signpost and foretaste of hope for the worldwide church today.

This book embodies Martin Kahler's dictum, "Mission is the mother of theology." It is here and now that we as denominations, seminaries, pastors, bishops, and laity are being called and sent by God to be missional, rather than to do maintenance church theology and practices. Pat Keifert is like a voice in the desert inviting local churches on a journey of spiritual discernment ". . . to move from the maintenance of Christendom to innovating missional church in their time and location."

This book is the fruit of Pat's personal and professional commitment with partners in mission in Southern Africa, Europe, and North America, as well as work that is breaking new ground on other continents. The practices and stories of local churches resound in Pat's lifelong work as patterns of what God is doing and where and with whom He is at work. As a dear friend and partner in God's mission, Keifert brought to our attention, ". . . we are in a time of change, perhaps epochal change in the relationships of church, gospel, and culture." This book should become one of the key resources for seminaries, ministers, and laity to discern what, where, who, and how the church should be in this New Missional Era.

DR. GORDON E. DAMES

Director of the Southern-Africa Institute for Missional Church and Senior Lecturer:
Department of Practical Theology and Missiology Faculty of Theology, Stellenbosch University

04400

If you think that there are easy answers and quick fixes for church revitalization, then this book is your worst nightmare—and of course it's exactly what you need. If you suspect that our churches need to go on a transforming journey—a spiritual journey of discernment, imagination, reflection, communication, faith, and action—then this book by veteran consultant and scholar Pat Keifert is just what you've been looking for. Pat radiates wisdom born of experience, and this book makes that wisdom clear and accessible.

BRIAN McLAREN
author/networker (brianmclaren.net)

Pastors and other church leaders thrive—personally and professionally—when we have ongoing collegial conversations that are culturally aware, theologically reflective, full of on-the-ground wisdom, and that provoke us toward risk-taking.

In *We Are Here Now* Pat Keifert offers all of that—and gives us a framework for embedding change deeply in our churches and shaping leadership teams that can innovate and sustain faithful, live-giving missional engagement in our diverse contexts.

We don't need another book of bright ideas or management and marketing finesse, so I am grateful for Keifert's pursuit of spiritual discernment, deep transformation, and the creative deployment of churches as agents of God's love.

REV. MARK LAU BRANSON, ED.D.
Homer Goddard Associate Professor of Ministry of the Laity at Fuller Theological Seminary, Pasadena, California

Partnership for Missional Church (PMC) outlined in *We Are Here Now* is not a blueprint but a process of discernment using a vast research data bank helping churches move beyond discipleship to apostleship. Because it involves changing the culture of the church and cannot easily be thrown together in a long-range plan, PMC emphasizes listening and moving slowly. It assumes at the outset that we don't have the answers. They must be discerned from within our congregation and community and revealed by the Holy Spirit. The theology and research is so solid!

JOHN STROMMEN, SR. PASTOR
Mt. Olivet-Plymouth, MN

In *We Are Here Now,* Patrick Keifert offers us a book describing an approach for congregations and churches that does justice to the mystery of God's presence and guidance and that reveals tools to help them grapple with and discern the concrete mission for which the Holy Spirit will equip them. Never have I seen an author so aware that Christ's Spirit is alive and available to those who will dwell in God's Word. Keifert combines that insight with practices that help us discover the divine energy that enables us to become humble and real—partners in God's mission in the context of our corporate and individual lives. Attentive to culture, the reality of churches, and God's presence, this is a book that is vitally needed.

WILLIAM R. BURROWS
Managing Editor, Orbis Books

At last someone who has a clue—actually many clues—how to put arms and legs on the missional vision. Professor Pat Keifert is not only one of the most articulate missional theologians of our day, but he also shares his vast practical knowledge on how to engage with this vision in local congregations. Everyone interested in doing missional theology will gain wisdom from this book. It is a necessary break-through in moving from missional theory to missional praxis.

DR FREDERICK MARAIS
BUVTON Institute, University of Stellenbosch, South Africa

If the culture of your congregation or judicatory is already mission-shaped, any book or consultancy will do just fine—which explains why so many consultancies have no more impact than any other nice program that is "done" . . . and then gone. Missional change that endures requires a transformational work of the Spirit. That is what Pat Keifert invites us into in *We Are Here Now.* For 25 years Pat has been working and refining ways of participating with the Spirit in creating missional cultures among God's people—bottom-up, not top-down—and applying the best of both Trinitarian missional theology and rigorous sociological practices. Don't miss this little, powerful book.

REV. JAMES E. MEAD, DMIN
Pastor to Pittsburgh Presbytery

WE ARE
HERE
NOW

A MISSIONAL JOURNEY OF
SPIRITUAL DISCOVERY

WE ARE HERE NOW

A NEW MISSIONAL ERA

PATRICK KEIFERT

CHURCH INNOVATIONS INSTITUTE, INC.
ST. PAUL, MINNESOTA

WE ARE HERE NOW: A NEW MISSIONAL ERA
A Missional Journey of Spiritual Discovery

Published by Church Innovations Institute, Inc.
1563 Como Avenue Suite 103
St. Paul, Minnesota 55108
www.churchinnovations.org

Scripture quotations unless otherwise marked are from the New Revised Standard Version Bible © 1989 Division of Christian Education of the National Council of the Churches of Christ in the United States of America. Used by permission.

First edition 2006
Cover and interior design: Lookout Design, Inc.
Interior illustrations by Nico Simpson

ISBN 10: 0-9777184-1-7
ISBN 13: 978-0-9777184-1-2
Printed in the United States of America
13 12 11 10 09   2 3 4 5 6 7 8

TO JEANETTE

friend, partner, spouse

CONTENTS

ACKNOWLEDGEMENTS

THIS BOOK REPRESENTS reflections upon 20 years of working with congregations and their local leaders. Therefore, the list of those to whom I owe much could go on for many pages. This short acknowledgement will not accomplish anything close to such recognition of my debt. Hopefully it will make clear some of the major contributors to this little book and what it represents in terms of more than 25 years of ministry.

First, I must thank some of the congregations that have given me life and partnership: Zion Lutheran Church, Rapid City, S.D. (my home congregation); Mt. Tabor Lutheran Church, Manchester, Mo. (Contextual Education in Seminary—no longer in existence); Mt. Olive Lutheran Church, Minneapolis, Minn. (my internship congregation); congregations I have served as pastor: First Lutheran Church of the Trinity, Chicago; Windsor Park Lutheran, Chicago; Pilgrim Evangelical Lutheran Church, Chicago; Galilee Lutheran Church, Roseville, Minn.; Lord of Life Lutheran Church, Renton, Wash.; Trinity Lutheran Church, Cody, Wyo.; Hope Lutheran Church, Powell, Wyo.; the original 13 congregations in the first cluster of Partnership for Worship and Evangelism in the Delaware-Maryland Synod of the Evangelical Lutheran Church in America, especially St. John's Lutheran, Columbia, Md., and its then pastor, Robert Wallace; the thousands of congregations that trusted me and Church Innovations staff in partnership in dozens of denominations and hundreds of judicatories on several continents.

Second, the staff, present and past, of Church Innovations Institute: Dr. Pat Taylor Ellison, David Stark, John Lonsbury, Judy

Stack-Nelson, John Hensrud, Kristie Hennig, Linda Budzien McEwen, Celeste Boda, Shirley Teig, Beth Maland, Linda Bergquist, Kevin Nicholson, Johanna Keifert, Mark Juel, Jerod Rauk, Danielle Keifert, Nathan Frambach, Scott Frederickson, Jon Case, Bruce Peterson, Jeanne Dahl, Jeanne Markquart, Scott Frederickson, John Mueller Nowell, Karen Stack, Les Bankson, Stephanie Veatch, Anita Bradshaw, Kristine Stache, Caroline Hvidsten, Jason Bryan-Wegner, Kyle Schiefelbein, Ben Cieslik, Brett Kosek, Jo Ellison, Slavka Gulanova, and Barbara Miller Fleischhaker.

Third, the Board of Trustees of Church Innovations Institute: the Right Rev. Mark MacDonald (chair); Bishop Callon Holloway (vice-chair); Marie Failinger, Esq. (secretary); Gordon Engstrom (treasurer/controller); the Rev. Gary Anderson; Linda Bergquist; the Rev. Wesley Granberg-Michaelson; the Rev. Dr. Donald H. Juel (+); the Rev. Hugh Magers; the Rev. John Strommen; Sarah Stegemoeller, Esq.; and the Rev. Bruce Modahl.

Fourth, associated consultants of Church Innovations Institute who have worked on Partnership for Missional Church: the Rev. Dr. Lois Barrett, Kyle McKenzie Nowell, the Rev. Dr. Alan Roxburgh, the Rev. Dr. Conrad Kanagy, the Rev. Mary Sue Dehmlow Dreier, the Rev. Anne Roser, the Rev. Patti Morlock, the Rev. Carl Johnson, the Rev. Craig Morton, the Rev. Dr. Gary Waller, and the Rev. Gordon Dames.

Fifth, I want to thank the institutions, foundations, and individuals who have supported Church Innovations's research into congregational leadership and transformation: The Lilly Endowment, Inc. (especially the Rev. Dr. Craig Dykstra and the Rev. Dr. James Wind), the Louisville Institute (especially the Rev. Dr. James Lewis), the Pew Charitable Trust, the Otto Bremer Foundation, and Aid Association for Lutherans. Among the individuals who will allow me to mention their names I especially want to thank Judy and John Bonnes who lent to and supported Church Innovations Institute when it was but a dream and have continued to support it with prayers, friendship, and finances.

Sixth, my colleagues in research deserve a deep thanks since they often offered their extraordinary intellectual gifts for little or no pay and with little or no sense of where or when their efforts would see the light of day. These include most importantly Donald H. Juel, who, despite the fact that Partnership for Missional Church continually took time from our work in hermeneutics and theological education, never complained and always supported the work of Church Innovations. Also, the Congregational Research Team, including Gary Simpson, David Frederickson, Nancy Hess, H. Kirk Hadaway, Michael Welker, Mark MacDonald, Ann O'Hara Graff (+), Cindy Jurrison, Lois Malcolm, and Ronald W. Duty, and more recently the International Research Consortium, including Coenie Burger, Pieter Grove, Will Storrar, Dirkie Smit, Harald Hegstad, Frederick Marais, James Wind, Don Browning, Hans Raun Iverson, Hijme Stoffels, Michael Herbst, and Stanley W. Green. I have also enjoyed the support of the Gospel and Our Culture Network worldwide, including some persons not mentioned above: Darrell Guder, Craig Van Gelder, Kent Miller, Dale Ziemer, Louise Johnson, George Hunsberger, and Alvin Luedke. None of them furthered their academic careers much by spending time on these topics, but they profoundly shaped the research and learning organization that is Church Innovations Institute.

Seventh, thanks to the valuable insights of members of the Yellowstone group not named elsewhere: James (Jim) Johnson, Timothy (Tim) Oslovich, Kathryn (Kathy) Brown, Renee AuMiller, Richard (Dick) Welscott, David (Dave) Mesaros, Mary Sharon Moore, Bruce Swanson, Gretel Van Wieren, Harold (Hal) Weldin.

Eighth, once in a long while one meets an artist who has remarkable skills with the art of cartoon. Once in a while one meets a theologian who gets your ideas and makes them clearer for more people. Once in a while one meets an educator who understands congregations and how they learn. Only once have I met all of these three in one person: Nico Simpson. I can only hope you spend as much time on his ironic humor that develops my prose as you do on my prose. It's worth the time and learning. Thank you, Nico.

Ninth, I want to thank the editorial team for this book: Pat Judd, consultant extraordinaire; Vicky Goplin, a superb and delightful editor and critic; and Mark Priddy, CEO of Allelon Publishing, who made this publication possible. Together with others this team can and will make a real difference in the liminal and emergent congregations seeking to walk into God's preferred and promised future in the New Missional Era.

Finally, I thank my family. When I speak in the book of my grieving the passing of Christendom, I speak especially of my mother, Ella (nee Rogers) Keifert, her mother, Erma (nee Larsen) Rogers, and their extended family and friends who raised me in the faith and surrounded me with a great cloud of witnesses to our Lord Jesus Christ. I thank my daughters, two of whom, Johanna and Danielle, worked for the Institute, and one, Sandra, who with her husband, Peter, contribute financially and emotionally to the work of the Institute regularly and faithfully. Most dearly, I thank my beloved friend and wife, Jeanette, who through her work as a physician makes my habit of running the Institute into debt fiscally possible, or close to possible. She prays, praises, critiques, and loves the work of Church Innovations and provides the emotional center for me even though I spend way too much time away from her.

WE ARE HERE NOW: INTRODUCTION

FOR MORE THAN 25 YEARS, I have worked with local churches in situations of high social stress and change. First, I worked as a pastor, and second, as a researcher and consultant. In most cases, I consider my work as a process of failure: excellent mistakes from which I learned that in turn led to some positive outcomes blessed by God.

On the basis of this process of failure turned into excellent mistakes, I invite you on a journey—a journey of spiritual discernment for local churches called to move from the maintenance of Christendom to innovating missional church in their time and location. This journey of spiritual discernment grows out of a great deal of experience working with local churches; so, while it has risks, you will benefit from these years of experience.

Indeed, I surely am not suggesting I am an exemplary leader of local church. The lion's share of my time, I have been a researcher and consultant, not a leader of a local church. Nonetheless, through most of those years, I was working on a regular basis with leaders of local churches. Some of the leaders were skilled and talented. Many knew that the church needed to change and that they did not know any easy answers to bring about that change.

As a consultant, I have used many of the models of change, tools, and books in the fields of local church development, redevelopment, church growth, evangelism, and mission. I have assumed that each of them has some insights, wisdom, and knowledge that might help the church be faithful to God's preferred future. Rather than first finding fault, I have sought to understand their strengths and point of view, and, if those strengths and point of view were compatible with a missional viewpoint, I risked along with those models and tools.

Although my first response to these many approaches has been one of understanding and appreciating their strengths and perspectives, I am a lifelong learner. As such, I have used my skills as a researcher, consultant, and theologian to critically reflect on these models, tools, and books. With other researchers, I have engaged in a deliberate, sustained, critical analysis of these models. As a systematic theologian I have sought to develop a coherent, relatively adequate theological framework for using these models. This seeking caused me to learn from the field of missiology, especially missiologists Lesslie Newbigin and David Bosch. Within their work, I have integrated a more traditional systematic theology following the dictum of the theologian Martin Kahler, "Mission is the mother of theology."

As a teacher in a seminary that educates thousands of leaders of local churches, I have wrestled and struggled to integrate what I am learning in my consulting and research into how I conceive of theological education and the theological framework for leadership development in the contemporary church.

As the founder and president of Church Innovations Institute, a nonprofit, church-related learning organization supported by a mix of individual gifts, foundational grants, and income from consultation work and publications, I have spent not a small amount of time imagining new ways of supporting and funding the development and redevelopment of local missional churches and the systems that support them.

From the late 1980s to the present time, I have guided the development of this journey of spiritual discernment for missional local churches and their support systems. Initially this journey was called "Project for Worship and Evangelism," then "Partnership for

Congregational Renewal," and most recently "Partnership for Missional Church"™ (PMC). What started as a handful of local churches in Delaware and Maryland has become a network of local churches on several continents involving dozens of denominations and cultures.

The sources of this work are varied, including India and southern Africa, Europe, and North America. With deep debts to the conversations of the Gospel and Our Culture Network from around the world, Partnership for Missional Church™ draws upon many sources, including and especially the thousands of local churches from whom our consulting and research has drawn most of its insights. To these many partners I offer a genuine thanks and a hope that this small book describing the present Partnership journey in light of its previous experiences of learning from failure might reflect a powerful portion of the wisdom and insights they have offered me and my colleagues at Church Innovations. I want to acknowledge a profound debt to Dr. Patricia Taylor Ellison, who has consistently sought to realize the lessons of our research in practical tools and processes.

I hope this little book creates in you the sense that you have partners in your desire to be missional church.

A NEW MISSIONAL ERA

AN OLD IRISH TALE GOES, "A man decides he wants to go to a very special place in the west of Ireland. Being a total stranger to Ireland, he decides to ask for directions. He asks the first knowledgeable looking stranger, someone who looks local, 'Can you tell me how to get to this place?' The local responds, 'Never heard of it. But if I were going there, I wouldn't start from here.'"

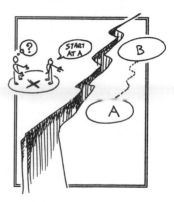

Silly as it may sound, I have found many books, consultants, church leaders, and pundits basically saying the same thing to congregations seeking to move beyond their present situation. They know that where they want to go is a special place, but they really don't know the lay of the land or how to get there, so they turn to these experts because they look like they are locals and know how to get to this special place. Most of these experts tell them they need to be a totally different church than they are. Most describe an "ideal" church, a church with 12 keys or 8 qualities, or a church that does worship or preaching or small groups just right and, of course, in a way totally different from the church asking the questions. From the point of view of the local church, these local-looking experts are saying, "If I were going there, I wouldn't start from here." They always point to a starting location off the map of most local churches. They point across a great gap and say, "either fill in the gap or somehow transport yourself across the gap to an ideal point."

Of course, missional church is a special place and time, and no one local church will embody the whole of missional church; it will never look exactly like that special place and time that God prefers and promises the whole church is and will be. The body of Christ is always greater than any local church. However, that is not the effect most of these "ideal" church books and pundits have on local church leaders trying to move from where they are to where God is calling them. The effect is to leave them feeling lost, and believing that if they want to get found, they need to start in a totally different place than they are at now.

WE ARE HERE NOW

The spiritual journey I am inviting you on is both a much more modest project than remaking your local church into a totally differ-

ent place and time than where and what you are now, and a much deeper and wider process than the dominant models of change being offered by most leaders on church renewal and development. This spiritual journey begins both with a much more positive assessment of your local church, of its capacities as Christian community, and a more radical and challenging understanding of the depth of change necessary for our time and place in Christian history. The journey begins by asking where and when are we in Christian history.

I promised to invite you on a spiritual journey. And so I will, but I am going to try to describe where we are first. I will describe our present "lay of the land" or situation in ways too broad to fit your situation exactly, but hopefully my description will be clear enough for you to get a sense of where you are within this description, clear enough for you to make an X on this map and write, "We are here now."

I invite you to put your own X on the map, not only because it makes sense to start where you are, but because I believe God provides all the gifts necessary for the future that God prefers and promises each local church. Unfortunately, most local churches either don't believe this or aren't interested, or don't know how to attend to those gifts; they fail to engage in the spiritual discernment of God's preferred and promised future.

Be that as it may, each journey begins where you are, not where you should be or where the ideal church is or should be. The journey begins with, "We are here now." So, where are we? What follows describes in very broad strokes the entire history of the church from the point of view of the local church and where most local churches are today.

HOW BAD IS IT?

In the last couple of decades, North Americans have heard some hyperbolic descriptions of our contemporary situation. Some call it postmodern, post-Christian, post-Constantinian, or post-Christendom. The style of this speech is often breathless, overwrought, fearful, and, too often, presumptuous. We hear about the once and future church, the ancient and future church, the seven-day-a-week church, the emergent church, and—my favorite—the missional church. The list could go on. How big is the change we are facing? How bad is it?

This hyperbolic language both is and is not warranted. The language sometimes reflects the genuine fears of the speakers. The language sometimes plays more to the fears of the audience.

More often than not, it builds a sense of community around a negative emotion rather than around shared positive faith in the promises
of God. It reinforces the message that we cannot ever get where we
want to go from where we are at the present moment. All that said,
this hyperbolic language is warranted because we are in a time of
change, perhaps epochal change in the relationships of church, gospel,
and culture. It is a change in time and location for the local church,
its immediate environment, and its greater cultural environment. The
change is big!

Many denominations are suffering tremendous transformation,
some downsizing, others growing, still others stagnant or in an in-
between state. Denominations designated mainline because of their
presence in the establishment of Protestant culture during the first
two centuries of the American republic face marginalization, forcing
them into major identity confusion and tremendous disaffection
among members. Denominations once designated as marginal or even
as cults now enjoy major influence in U.S. civil and political life.

 Others are holding still, or stagnating, or
feeling confused about who they are and
where they fit within the cultural scene of
contemporary North America.

This change among denominations parallels
major change for many local churches. Changes in their immediate
environment cause tremendous stress. Local churches that expect
membership to hold or grow on the basis of denominational loyalty
stagnate, decline, or die. Congregations that were used to resources in
their immediate environment—family, schools, other nonprofit
organizations—that once provided support and many of the practices
of making disciples of Jesus Christ flounder in this new environment.
Those that come from a tradition that does not depend upon such
support in the immediate environment or have learned how to form
Christian community out of their own resources now flourish.

All of this change, whether at the local or denominational church level, merits hyperbolic speech for almost all circumstances. Some very important things are changing in the relationship of gospel, church, and culture. However, I find language such as post-  Christian or postmodern simply too extreme for the situation. Indeed, any observation of the North American scene sees an emergent struggle between (1) the so-called "naked public square," (2) the diversity of religious voices, and (3) a growing engagement of Christians with civil and public life. While Christianity in North America has undergone several disestablishments in the last 200 years, it is hard to see the present culture devoid of Christian influence in its woof and warp. Indeed, most religious voices are growing in their influence on civil and public life, especially Christian voices.

WORLD CHRISTIANITY

More importantly, an emerging world Christianity, especially in Africa, Asia, and South America, leaves even the casual observer with the impression that the 21st century is as likely as the 20th century to be a Christian century. Post-Christian sounds to me like the ranting of mainliners used to presumptive importance, or the predictions of overly triumphant secularists, or the expressions of hope of the growing number of faithful of other religions rather than a sober observation of the current scene in North America and internationally. Neither North America nor the international scene appears post-Christian.

The changes internationally are sometimes described as postmodern; this also seems too much. We certainly are in a new moment in modernity, a time when the great experiments and hopes of the

European Enlightenment are coming under a needed critique. This time is a reflective moment that recognizes how European were the Enlightenment's methods and modes. I find most of what is labeled postmodern, however, to be more a combination of this much-needed reflection and criticism with some of the modes and methods of pre-modern cultures, including European.

What I see taking place for example in Africa is not so much post-modern as it is many diverse cultures emerging forcefully into the contemporary global realities that are profoundly shaped by European-American modernity. The emergent "indigenous" African churches reflect more a struggle of traditional cultures with European modernity than a postmodernity. Even if there is a phenomenon we can call postmodern, most persons experience a mixture of modern and postmodern life.

Even if you want to retain this hyperbolic "post" language, each of these "post" images clearly focuses not on the future but on the past by engaging in a negative definition of the present. For analytic pur-poses, for understanding our past and present situation, this is helpful. For engaging in planning and acting into God's preferred and prom-ised future, "post" language is probably not as helpful as some of its proponents believe.

I prefer a much more positive, hopeful, and challenging descrip-tion of our situation: a "New Missional Era." This New Missional Era shapes Partnership for Missional Church™. PMC sees the end of the last century inaugurating a New Missional Era around the world. This New Missional Era takes very different shapes in different cultures, but some broad generalizations seem worth making.

In some ways, this New Missional Era reflects significant and deep change in Western European and North American culture. The Era also reflects sweeping worldwide developments in Christian mission. In the case of most of the world, Christianity during the last decades has flourished, while in North America many local Christian churches have remained on a plateau or lost ground in worship attendance, membership, and engagement in their mission and ministry. Of course, not all local churches fit within this pattern of holding or diminishing. Indeed, some local churches and some denominations are strengthening in breadth and depth of engagement with North American culture.

The general pattern in Western Europe, however, is increasingly grim. Protestant Europe has long seen very low percentages of church participation, and recent decades have seen similar patterns among Catholics. In the face of these patterns, many have talked about the end of Christendom. Before going any further, it might be helpful to understand what is meant by Christendom before talking about its end. What follows is an extremely short history of the church from the point of view of the local church.

THE APOSTOLIC AGE

The Christian movement that followed the death, resurrection, and ascension of our Lord Jesus Christ emerged by the power of the Holy Spirit and was given to the apostles, the disciples, and followers of Jesus who were sent by Jesus into the world. The local churches these apostles founded grew out of the dispersed Jewish community in the ancient Græco-Roman Empire and grew modestly in some locations and more rapidly in others.

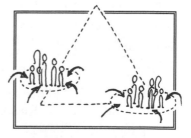

The local church found itself at once dependent upon the Jewish community and its synagogues and also increasingly alienated and even persecuted by the same Jewish community. From the point of view of most inhabitants of the ancient Græco-Roman Empire, the emerging Christian movement was seen as a part of the Jewish religion.

Local churches experienced a mission field on all sides of their lives, even in the midst of their weekly gatherings in houses. These house churches included a mixture of Jews, proselytes to the emerging Judaism, and God-fearing seekers. In some locations and some times, the local church was forced to hide its identity and carry on its worship and ministry in secret. Even where persecution was rare and the local church could meet without much fear of harm, the local house churches did not have to go anywhere to find their mission field. Everywhere they turned they experienced persons to whom they were sent to initiate into the reign of God. This was true within and without the local church.

Being missional

This Apostolic Age was characterized by local churches understanding themselves to be mission outposts within the mission of God; communities called, gathered, and sent in God's mission, the very movement of God toward the world. "Even as the Father has sent me, so I send you" (John 20:21). They found themselves caught up into God's movement and life. They did not imagine mission as something or somewhere other than their primal activity as a called, gathered, centered, and sent people of God. This is the core characteristic of a missional church: being, not just doing, mission.

Being, not just doing, mission focused not so much on bringing people to church—some identified building—but being the church in, with, and under the friends, neighbors, coworkers, and strangers of people's everyday lives. As a result, the church did not have "a mission" apart from its very identity because being church was

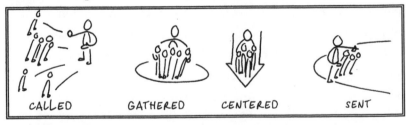

CALLED   GATHERED   CENTERED   SENT

being missional; being church was being called, gathered, centered, and sent within the life of God for the sake of God's mission in the world. Of course, most local churches were not this way all the time, perhaps not even most of the time, but they were this way enough of the time to become a powerful movement in the ancient world.

Theology and doctrine

Out of this situation of being called, gathered, and sent across boundaries where Jesus had not yet gone, theology and doctrine arose. Indeed, mission was the mother of theology and doctrine. Early theology and doctrine grew out of the process of giving Christian answers to the frequently asked questions (FAQs) of a particular community. The written Christian answers to FAQs became the first catechisms. These catechisms, combined with glosses on Christian scriptures, homilies and sermons, prayers, hymns, and the ritual practices of the Christian community, became the sources of subsequent doctrinal and creedal development.

Since that ancient world was intensely diverse in culture, religion, language, government, and economics, theology and doctrine were equally diverse. For the local church, this meant a need to form and shape its own Christian identity without an appeal to some presupposed consensus of support from the immediate environment. The local church survived on its own resources and its own ability to grow community around a clearly defined identity.

Even as late in this period as A.D. 402, a large local church, like the one in the seaside city of Hippo, could afford a full-time bishop who was, as scriptures say, "apt to teach." In the case of Hippo, this bishop had a congregation of perhaps 100 with worship attendance around 60. He spent his time teaching the primary pastoral caregivers, the 12 elders of the congregation, who must have carried out a house church or small group form of ministry between gatherings of the whole community on Sundays. He was to become the most influential teacher in the emerging Latin church, that part of the church we call Christendom. His name, as you might already know, was Aurelius Augustine, St. Augustine.

CHRISTENDOM

Beginning in the time of Augustine, the Latin and Greek churches moved further and further apart. As the Roman Empire divided between Old Rome (Latin West) and New Rome (Constantinople, the Greek East), the dire straits of Old Rome forced the church to take on more and more of the task of maintaining culture. This was true from the time of Augustine onward.

With the rise of Islam, first in the East and then throughout northern Africa and eventually parts of what we now call Spain and Italy, the New Rome became isolated from the Old Rome, surrounded by pagan Slavs and the new religion of the Koran. This hastened the need for the church in the Latin West to preserve and sustain civilization as they knew it. In short, almost all the tasks of maintaining Western culture became tasks of the church.

If you wanted to become a doctor, you went to the church; if you wanted to become a lawyer, you went to the church; even the development of warriors became invested with Christian commitments in the movement of knights. Music, mathematics, politics, medicine, and law became the business of the church. By A.D. 800, a Pope crowned a new Holy Roman Emperor. The formation of Christendom, a fusion of Christianity and civil kingdom—Christendom—was complete.

For the local church, this meant a new reality of the parish and parish pastor. The Christian parish was a political and geographical area within which each person, except the rare Jew or Muslim, was considered a member. Within this political geographical area, all residents were presumed members of the flock and required, as a result, a parish shepherd, a parish pastor. The parish pastor's responsibility was to maintain the flock: to hatch, match, and dispatch the members. Evangelism and mission became relatively irrelevant. Evangelism was done by the parishioners

having babies. Financial support of this parish pastor depended on the complex systems of the political-geographical princes and bishops, but not the members of the local parish.

Between 800 and 1648 the business of European Western culture and the business of the church were relatively indistinguishable. To be sure, the missionary movements north and east of the Rhine incorporated more and more Europeans into Christendom. This incorporation into Christendom required brave, determined, and smart missionaries, most drawn from missionary orders. Eventually most of Europe became Christendom.

For all of its call for change, radical and otherwise, the Reformation of the 16th century did not truly change this situation. Indeed, in some ways, the centuries-old struggle between church and state, pope and prince, seemed to be leaning in Protestant lands toward the prince, but the separation of prince and church was yet to happen. Indeed, the attempt to resolve the governance issue by the principle of "as the ruler believes, so go the ruled" became the source of tremendous suffering.

DISESTABLISHMENT OF THE CHURCH

First disestablishment

In no small part, the birth of modernity (1650–1950) grew out of the desire to end religious wars by grounding political life upon pure reason and objective facts rather than the profound but irrational dogmas of religion. This eventually led to the separation of church and state, one of the primary achievements of modernity. It is no accident that the first of the freedoms enunciated in the First Amendment to the U.S. Constitution clarifies both the free exercise of religion and the disestablishment of any state religion. And, although it would take until 1825 and 1827 in the states of Massachusetts and Connecticut for the Congregational Church finally to give up establishment, this action began the first of three major disestablishments of religion in the United States.

Second disestablishment

For the local church, the first disestablishment meant very little for many decades in most communities where the Protestant church in its various forms maintained a de facto establishment, a kind of "folks church" or community church. Roman Catholics refused to give way to the illusion of cultural disestablishment, especially in places where they created a critical mass. They refused to send their children to so-called public schools where the Protestant establishment ruled, founding a substantial parochial school movement instead. With their movement into the political and economic establishment in the early 20th century, the de facto Protestant folks church experienced a second disestablishment.

Third disestablishment

Following the Second World War, a third disestablishment of the church took place with the greater recognition of Jewish religious traditions. The idea of the Judeo-Christian tradition of American and

Western culture entered the lexicon. This third disestablishment has continued with a growing Muslim presence and, since 1965, the religions of the East have created a diversity of religious life and practice for many North Americans. Many mainline Christians find themselves, like my family, living among Hindus, Muslims, Jews, Buddhists, agnostics, and secularists, along with growing numbers of articulate conservative evangelicals, charismatics, and Pentecostals as family, friends, coworkers, and neighbors. This diversity continues unabated in North America.

For the local congregation, this three-stage disestablishment has looked very different depending on geography and demography. Folks churches, in some cases, remain alive and well. I have worked with a number of Lutheran and Baptist churches that remain the "community church" for their location. New folks churches are being born in some communities, especially in recent immigrant communities. Korean Presbyterians, Chinese Baptists, and Peruvian Pentecostals are three emerging folks churches I have had the privilege of serving and learning from. Indeed, new immigrant church development remains one of the most underdeveloped and potentially fruitful fields of the New Missional Era in North America.

For most local churches, however, the experience of disestablishment has meant challenge, change, stress, and struggle. Those traditions that are most dependent upon the patterns of folks church are the most stressed. They expect the community, schools, families, and neighborhood nonprofit organizations to provide the social pressure, encouragement, and expectation to be Christian. They presume that the immediate environment will provide some of the primary practices of Christian belief, like teaching the Ten Commandments (or, at least, thinking the Ten Commandments are important for everyone) and honoring the Golden Rule, the value (if not the practice) of prayer, the rough outline of a church year as a normal way of understanding time (with Christmas and Easter being at least understood as important), Sunday closing laws, no extracurricular activities on Sunday morning, and so on.

Such congregations continue to expect their immediate environment to provide the primary resources for making Christians, forming disciples, and forming Christian community. In my experience, clergy who are functioning in the Christendom folks-church system complain that the young adults in their confirmation and youth ministry are biblically illiterate; ritually incompetent; highly suspicious of the church and church authority, especially of the clergy; highly self-conscious in a church atmosphere; struggling with family and school issues; and less than docile in the church environment. The list of complaints could and does go on. All of these complaints I shared as a teacher of catechism and Bible school. And I have come to one simple piece of advice for myself and other such church leaders: Get over it!

GRIEVING THE LOSS
OF CHRISTENDOM

Easier said than done, of course. Yes, grieve the loss of Christendom. I am not one of those consultants who want to dance on the grave of Christendom. I am a child of it, in some modest ways. But, to tell you the truth, I grew up not so much in a post-Christendom environment as a pre-Christendom environment in the inter-mountain West of the United States. Religion in general was considered something for women, children, and other weaklings. If you were over 14 and a male, the easiest way you could prove you were a man and not a child was to stop going to church. I am almost the only male in my extended family who attends church regularly and, as my Uncle Ralph has noted more than once, "You wear a dress on Sunday morning!" In my childhood, less than 12 percent of the community participated, even nominally, in a religious community. The pioneer spirit lived on, although of course romantically, even into my generation. No, my Christendom was tied deeply to a recognition of minority status, a way of being in the world that most of my friends and some of my relatives did not share. To be a Protestant Christian was odd, though tolerated. Although no doubt better than being a Catholic or a Jew, my Christian identity was best left in a private space.

Still, I grieve the loss of Christendom. I grew up singing German Lutheran chorales, often *auf Deutsch*. This was not a distinction of class but of culture. This music still remains my soul music. Its passing out of most churches in the New Missional Era grieves me deeply. I grieve the loss of grandmothers and mothers like mine who taught me to pray, who put the scriptures into my hands, who explained the everyday reality of life in terms of the scriptural narrative, who sat beside me in church, who ran their fingers under the liturgy in the service book so that I became literate in the liturgy long before I learned to read in school, who reviewed my memorization of Scripture and catechism most Friday nights of my early adolescent years in preparation for Saturday morning catechism classes. I grieve the loss of aunts and uncles, great aunts and great uncles who took all of this seriously in their lives and in mine, whose joy in this way of life was and is contagious, who did all of this, not because they felt some duty (though they no doubt felt duty), but because they wanted to pass on to me what gave them life, what made possible hope in their own really dark, hard, passionate, and purposeful lives.

When I think of Christendom, I think of these people and prac-tices in relationship with the local church and its pastor, but driven quite clearly by an ongoing tradition that gave these people life. I think of Mr. Classen, my public school sophomore biology teacher and a member of my congregation, who at the end of one class period said, "We will be teaching Darwinian evolution in this class. I know some of you might find this difficult to put together with your faith. I would invite you to meet with me after school to discuss how this theory of evolution can be related to the Bible and Christian faith."

He said it once. He met with a few of us, usually only two or three, and talked about how he put together his understanding of Darwinian evolution with Genesis 1–2. I have changed my mind about how he interpreted Genesis, and I have changed my mind about how he interpreted evolution. But no other person, including some world-renown philosophers and theologians with whom I have studied, so profoundly and thoroughly shaped my theological imagination as Mr. Classen did. He carried on a clear act of Christendom by connecting that informal class with his teaching of the sophomore biology class. I find it strange, even perverse, that anyone could dance on that grave. Although I realize that such mothers and grandmothers, aunts and uncles, and sophomore biology teachers are rare and that the culture in which they were common is, at least for the time being, gone with the wind, I still grieve their passing.

A NEW MISSIONAL ERA

Healthy grieving frees us for healthy new visions. Healthy grieving makes possible seeing the New Missional Era for what it is: God's invitation to join in this new adventure in the life of God and world, gospel, church, and culture. And, as deeply as I grieve, I more deeply delight in this new adventure. Partnership for Missional Church™ looks at this time around the world, including North America, and says "yes" to a partnership with God in this new era of the mission of God.

This is God's mission, not ours. This is God's mission and not just the church's, for it is the reign of God that is near, not just the church. The reign of God is far more than the church, though of course the church continuously experiences the breaking in of the reign of God. Imagine the reign of God as the space and time, will and movement of God that is at hand (but not in hand), that is present and creating the church but always more than, and even at times over against, the church and culture.

In this New Missional Era, this time of the missional church, those congregations that are faithful, effective, and efficient will be a part of transforming mission. They will be transformed by the mission—called, gathered, and centered in Word and sacrament, and sent into the mission of God in daily life.

This calling, gathering, centering, and sending crosses boundaries—boundaries established by powers and principalities often greater than even the will of all people, but most often exercised by the will of all people. In our time, these boundaries might be crossed by living out the biblical theme of hospitality to the stranger. But now I am getting ahead of myself; we are just describing where we are now.

Remember, "We are here now." We are in a time of Big Change. Christendom for most of us has passed; some of us who value its blessings grieve, and we should. Many of us have not noticed its passing. Some, very few, still live in locations and social environments where a folks church form of Christendom remains. However, most of us mark our Xs on the map of the history of Christianity at "Post-Christendom." Hopefully, you will also place that X in a time of New Missional Era for your local church.

PRIMING THE PUMP

If we could put our X on the "missional map," where would we be?

In terms of our church's mission, how would our longtime members describe us?

How would people outside our community describe us?

What do these answers tell us?

CHAPTER 2

MODELS OF CHANGE

PARTNERSHIP FOR MISSIONAL CHURCH™ strikingly differs from most proposals for congregational development and mission enhancement because it is grounded in spiritual discernment that focuses on cultural change and mission transformation. PMC transforms mission by engaging congregations primarily as cultural systems rather than as organizations. Transforming mission true to the gospel and the New Missional Era will transform culture and bring forth organizational change within that culture.

Indeed, introducing a lot of organizational change into a congregation can actually create such a negative response that the congregation loses any energy for the deep transforming process. A few examples should help point out the striking difference between most proposals based on organizational models and the PMC proposal based on cultural innovation.

ORGANIZATIONAL VS CULTURAL CHANGE

BEYOND WORSHIP WARS

You have probably heard the claim that the secret to church growth is offering seeker-sensitive worship services, or contemporary worship, or at least an alternative to the traditional worship of the congregation. Perhaps you have seen congregations visit some megachurch or church development seminar only to return home to introduce "alternative" worship.

In some cases, introducing alternative worship makes powerful connections for the people being served in mission—effectively, faithfully, and efficiently expanding the number of people served in mission. More often than not, however, introducing alternative worship leads to worship wars, a culture clash related to worship. Introducing alternative worship without engaging change either in the culture of the congregation or in the culture of the new group to be served in mission leaves the congregation and the persons it might serve in worse shape than before the introduction of alternative worship. Why? Introducing alternative worship is organizational change, not cultural transformation; it involves changing some practices, but it usually involves no spiritual discernment.

On the other hand, when a congregation introduces alternative worship by fully engaging the culture it seeks to serve, and when it opens itself to the cultural transformation of its existing community, something powerful and synergistic happens. Over the years, I have studied both kinds of congregations; there are congregations of all sizes and persuasions of doctrine, worship, and politics that get this right and that get this wrong. Some get it right intentionally, most accidentally. PMC assists congregations to do it intentionally, thus lowering the risk of worship wars and upping the chance of transforming mission.

Imagine a congregation in a central city location, the product of ethnic immigration from northern Europe in the late 19th century. Indeed, the congregation has been the mother of dozens of other congregations throughout the 20th century. Following World War II, the congregation became a center of liturgical renewal. Since the late

1960s, the congregation has steadily lost active members, and those who still attend continue to grow older, failing to pass their faith practices onto their children who remain within the city. Many of their children move elsewhere, sometimes to other cities and, more often than not, to the suburbs.

In the face of this decline, the congregation practices decades of adaptive denial regarding this profound change in its own culture and the surrounding community. Rather than finding God's movement in the changes of their neighborhood, church leaders primarily see these changes as signs of decline and, alas, more evidence of the devil than God. To put it bluntly, they seem more willing to ask, "What in Hades's name is going on here?" than to ask, "What in Heaven's name is going on here?" This failure to attend to the mission of God in their community usually accompanies blaming the community and various "others" for these terrible changes. "If the government hadn't put in that highway, we would still have a great location." "If the county hadn't built that halfway house in the neighborhood, our children would still be here on Sundays." "If the police would keep the drug dealers out of our neighborhood, we would still be a great church."

After decades of this adaptive denial, things come to a crisis. Previous generations had generously supported the excellent maintenance of buildings, staff, and endowment. This generosity now runs low, and the congregation can no longer maintain the size and quality of staff and buildings. After generations of mature and experienced pastors, the congregation can only attract a young and inexperienced pastor. The new pastor challenges the call committee to undergo a "radical change for mission." Attending conferences sponsored by his church's evangelism leadership, he accepts the conclusion that to reach younger and diverse groups of people, the church needs "seeker sensitive" and "contemporary" worship. The call committee agrees with him.

After a few months of honeymoon, he presents his plans for "contemporary" worship to the church council. The council is quite

divided. Some welcome the experiment. Some are willing to try anything that might mean institutional survival. Others seem unclear.
The most vocal and generally most influential are clearly opposed.
They either have joined the congregation recently or been long-time
members precisely because of its commitment to liturgical renewal.

The majority agree to try the contemporary service. They agree to
place it at a different time than the traditional liturgical service. The
liturgical crowd doesn't like it but allows the experiment. The council
appoints a group of members, suggested by the pastor, to put together
a contemporary service. This group attends a worship and evangelism
conference with a couple of churches in their community that are
"growing." With a few changes, they adopt a worship service used by
a fast-growing nondenominational church. They announce the first
Sunday contemporary worship service. A significant number of
persons from the traditional service attend, along with those who have
been calling for a contemporary service. The numbers are surprisingly
small, but they are committed.

After a year of the experiment, numbers in the contemporary
service have not grown and numbers in the traditional service have
continued to drop. Anxiety in the system goes up, and those committed to the liturgical service declare the experiment a failure. Those
committed to the contemporary service simply say that the worship
time was wrong and the service needs to be livelier with a different
style of music. The experimenters, strongly supported by the pastor,
succeed in changing the times of the worship services, hoping to
attract more people from the neighborhood. This move simply goes
too far for the traditional service crowd. The traditional crowd notes
that they gave the experiment a year and that is enough. It failed; it's
time to move on. The conflict moves from a tense agreement to experiment to an open conflict.

Some of the traditional crowd simply note that their way is the
tradition of the congregation and the experimenters should leave and

experiment on their own. Some others of the traditional crowd leave for another congregation that has already gone through a worship war, with the traditional side winning. Now the experimenters have a clear majority and put their time change into place. This move leads to bitter responses from those in the traditional service and no significant growth among the contemporary service crowd.

Without much fanfare, the congregation now has two worship services with fewer in worship than when they began the experiment. The members, filled with both anger and despair, continue putting their primary focus upon themselves and their differences. The community remains mostly secondary in their minds, and their ability to support the ministry of a traditional full-time pastor ends. They feel damned if they do and damned if they don't.

Through all this experimenting, they never attended in any intentional and deep way to their own culture, or the cultures of the immediate community, or the deeper spiritual questions. In all of this change they did not ask, "What is God calling us to do?" They did not ask, "What is God up to in this community?" Nor did they ask, "What is the useable future in our past?" They did not listen to or seek the hospitality of their "new" neighbors. They did not wonder in prayer, fasting, conversation and struggle, study and reflection, "What part of God's mission in this community is God calling us to do?" They experimented with organizational change through changing the structure of worship but did not discover the theological, spiritual, and cultural opportunities of their missional situation.

BEYOND SMALL GROUP TECHNOLOGY

Introducing small groups as organizational change is a pretty close second in popularity to introducing alternative worship. Over the past 30 years or so, we have watched one small group model

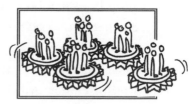

after another pass through the church. Most follow a particular method for introducing small groups and/or provide a pattern of curriculum and organization. Sometimes these work spectacularly; most often they do not.

After years of research and reflection on these patterns, we at Church Innovations Institute began to see that introducing small group ministry as organizational change rather than spiritual discernment that engages the culture created the same unnecessary and usually devastating conflict, harming both the existing community and those new persons intended to be served by small groups. The difference between organizational versus cultural change best explains the difference between success and failure in introduction and growth of small group ministry. The use of significant relational groups (the terminology of church consultant and theologian Kennon Callahan) as a strategy for ministry that diffuses missional innovation differs profoundly from small group ministry as curriculum or tactic within a church growth technology of organization. The problem is not in the small group ministry but in the method of introduction.

Imagine a large congregation of a once-immigrant tradition that has become a well-established mainline, middle class, suburban congregation. The congregation's senior pastor has just retired, leaving a legacy of general well-being, although leaders have noted steady decline in worship attendance and steady increase in median age. Without any intentional interim ministry, the congregation calls a highly successful "big church" pastor well-known for his books on church growth, including well-received books on small group ministry.

This pastor arrives from a very different culture, both church and regional. He is used to a high degree of freedom in appointing staff, functioning as the CEO of a small corporation. He inherits this more traditional, though larger, church that works with a more collegial model of staff and lay leadership. He takes leaders, both staff and lay, to a major church growth conference focusing on, among other things, introducing small group ministry.

Initial response from staff to small group ministry is very positive. They have been looking forward to change and this seems just the change they need. They begin to put the new organizational structure into place in their own work and in the areas of ministry they each direct.

Lay leaders give the senior pastor his honeymoon rights, although they are not at all enthusiastic. They have already seen a couple of small group curriculums or programs pass through the congregation working to some degree or another with small numbers of members. One small group program appealed to members who were part of the charismatic renewal movement. Another small group program appealed to some youth and young adults. They assume this small group ministry, too, will have that limited place in the life of the congregation.

The senior pastor and most of the programmatic staff push the introduction of the new organizational structure with great energy and enthusiasm. The early adopters within the membership tend to be those who have recently joined the congregation or those who were quite alienated from the previous pastor and his regime. The vast majority of the congregation ignores the attempts to introduce the new organizational structure of ministry. However, a small but influential group of lay and staff leaders resent what they see as an "imposition" of a foreign culture upon their church.

Having a very passive-aggressive culture, the congregation hides its level of resentment well in failure to participate—at least for the length of the honeymoon. The honeymoon, unfortunately, comes to an end with a bang. Not a full year after the first church growth conference and the introduction of its organizational changes, the resentment appears on the surface. First, the resentment explodes in the middle of the yearly congregational meeting like a torpedo exploding amidships. Second, many of the staff supervisory committees that endured attempts to turn them into small groups began to openly reject these attempts. Staff members most committed to introducing small group ministry receive negative reviews.

Before he knows how deep and wide the resentment and resulting anger is, the new senior pastor realizes that most of the new leaders elected at the annual congregational meeting intend to remove him. Staff members he recruited are at risk as well. Staff that had passively agreed to his changes now openly speak out against the changes. Within six months, he and the new staff are gone—he to an early but comfortable retirement, they to whatever jobs they can find.

At this same time this was all happening, we at Church Innovations were researching this congregation in considerable depth. We were able to trace the deep cultural conflict this organizational change approach brought to the surface. Without the spiritual practices for opening leadership to discernment of God's preferred future, most leaders and active members of the congregation experienced the organizational change as the imposition of a new elite who had not earned their trust. Without listening deeply to the culture of the congregation and its surrounding community, the new pastor guaranteed both this culture clash and his inability until too late to recognize it and respond effectively to it.

This same pattern of introducing small group ministry without a process of spiritual discernment and attending to culture has created similar disasters in smaller congregations. Indeed, the pattern is more obvious in smaller congregations because they tend to be run by one group of insiders. Without spiritual discernment and attention to culture, insider groups most often see the introduction of small group ministry as a significant threat to their own leadership.

Imagine a small rural congregation that calls a new pastor. The new pastor had come to Christian faith through a small group in college. During seminary she had started a small group for support and for study. Now she arrives in her first call in this small rural congregation anticipating the delight of starting small group ministry in the local church.

She begins by starting a small group to provide support for her in her ministry. Aside from one long-time member, recently widowed, all the members of the small group are new to the local church. Existing leaders allow a honeymoon but clearly are nervous about this new group that has so much influence on their pastor.

Six months later, the pastor starts another small group around a matter of deep concern to her. Once again, this group represents a threat to the existing power structures, but those power brokers do not say a word, not a word to the pastor. They do, however, start to pass their concerns along to other influence brokers in the congregation. After 18 months, they succeed in recalling the pastor.

This pattern in smaller churches was so common in our research that some 15 years ago we developed a separate model for introducing small groups to small churches. This same research provided important insights into the difference between organizational versus cultural models of change. In this research, we began to see the breadth of the need for spiritual discernment as culture is engaged.

BEYOND CONFLICT MANAGEMENT

By now you are probably making a mental list of other examples of alternative organizational models for congregational governance or staff configurations. You might be thinking, "What was really needed in the above instances was conflict intervention." And I am quite willing to agree with you that each of  these instances could have used good conflict intervention.

Most models of conflict intervention, however, depend on organizational and psychological models of the congregation. Some of these models, especially those dependent upon family systems theory, can

lower the anxiety of the congregational system (a major accomplishment!), but they simply do not address the diffusion of innovation in
a culture. At best, they lower anxiety to a point where some other
resources might address the change of culture; at worst, they tranquil-
ize the congregation, offering it a peace that fails to address the
mission and purpose of the local church and allows the congregation
to drift, decline, or even die peacefully. In short, these family systems
based models of conflict intervention may prevent total meltdown,
but they abet and encourage adaptive denial. In the end, they prevent
a healthy engagement with the deeper cultural and spiritual issues
facing the local church in the New Missional Era.

GAP VS DIFFUSION
OF INNOVATION

The most obvious difference between the PMC model of change
and the dominant practices in the church is the contrast between a
gap model and a diffusion of innovation model as developed by
Everett Rogers. In the gap model, change is understood as taking place
within a linear model of causality. In the figure below, T1 is the point
of intervention and T2 is the point in time the intervention is
expected to be successful.

In most cases, this model of change in the church begins at T1
with an evaluation of the congregation, using some agreed-upon list
of characteristics, keys, qualities, or patterns of a successful, healthy,
growing, effective, pick-your-positive-term church. Needless to say,
upon evaluation, most congregations find themselves wanting. Some

may score higher than others; some may be motivated to change; many, when evaluated, are not motivated to change but rather experience considerable shame and guilt. Most that are motivated to change introduce organizational change to address the absence of the desired characteristics, keys, qualities, or patterns. This organizational model perceives the challenge as a gap between present practices and desired practices.

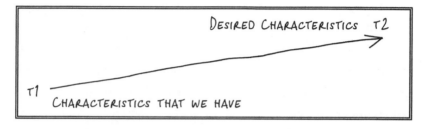

DESIRED CHARACTERISTICS T2

T1

CHARACTERISTICS THAT WE HAVE

CHARACTERISTICS THAT WE HAVE

The task then is to design a strategic, long-range plan to fill the gap. Intermediate goals, a road map for marking milestones, and timelines noting who is responsible for achieving these goals are committed to paper in a document. And, as one woman said to me, more often than not, "it goes on the shelf of good intentions."

Very recently a young woman with a decade or so of business experience in a Fortune 500 company and an MBA from a prestigious university business school used her skills for the sake of her local church. She took leaders through a state-of-the-art strategic planning process and completed what I considered an excellent strategic plan. I was so impressed that I asked for a copy to share with other congregations. As I was explaining to her the difference between organizational and cultural models of change, her face lighted up.

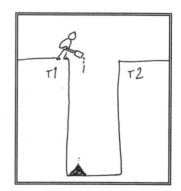

"No wonder I was so proud of the plan but knew there was almost nobody in the congregation willing to do it," she blurted out. As she continued to reflect, she realized that if an organization has a well-established culture of receiving a strategic plan as the means to accomplish an agreed-upon objective within a shared sense of mission, then a strategic plan works beautifully. Absent that shared sense of mission—a deep cultural reality—strategic plans, no matter how well gathered and formed, fail to gain the commitment of energy, time, and resources for transforming mission.

PMC is different. It works with a diffusion-of-innovation understanding of how cultures change. This model, while enjoying a couple generations of wide endorsement in the field of cultural anthropology, represents a major innovation within models of congregational development. We came to this model mostly from theological reflection on 18 years of experience of working with local churches in clusters. These clusters of local churches would commit themselves to a three- to five-year process for moving from maintenance to mission. Over

time, we began to see a basic difference between those local churches that found the process productive and those that didn't. Those that clearly did were following a diffusion-of-innovation process addressing the culture of the congregation and not just the organization of it. Upon theological reflection, we saw that the principles of the Gospel and Our Culture movement started by Lesslie Newbigin seemed right on target.

The diffusion-of-innovation model, developed by social scientist Everett Rogers, follows a fairly simple set of patterns that are, of course, profoundly complex. He argues that change seldom takes place between point A to point B along a straight, clear timeline. No, indeed, change follows a fairly unpredictable path and enjoys multiple causes for each event, including causes located in the future and not merely in the past. The path appears more like the journey of a sailboat than that of a train, plane, or automobile.

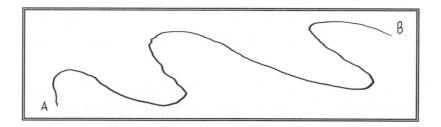

STAGES OF DIFFUSION OF INNOVATION

Rogers names different moments within this diffusion-of-innovation process. While these moments appear on a line of movement, they do not take place in a purely linear manner; indeed, they proceed in a diversity of movement but do depend upon one another and require a certain level of achievement in each stage to make possible the next.

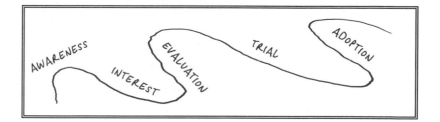

AWARENESS

In the town where I live, we have fairly violent thunderstorms, even tornadoes. One of the ways we warn people about an approaching storm is a cold war leftover: the air raid siren. These sirens are truly obnoxious and thus hard to ignore. Nonetheless, when they first sound, I find myself not noticing them immediately. It takes a while for me to become aware of their disturbing sound.

So goes cultural change. Even as profound and disturbing as it can be, it happens often without people being aware of it. It happens behind our backs. The beginning of our response to change is becoming aware of the change. Often in the case of the cultural change regarding the relationship between the gospel and our culture, it helps to have someone interpret a number of changes so that they begin to fit a shared explanation. This initial stage in PMC uses various tools and processes to bring about awareness. During this first stage, we look for leaders who have a growing awareness of the change and share in our explanation for this change.

INTEREST

Back to the air raid siren. When the siren goes off and I slowly become aware of it, it takes me a bit to move from awareness to interest in this alarming sound. I go from noting the noise to reminding myself that it means danger.

This movement from awareness to interest takes quite a while for many in the church. Initially some notice the difference between how some congregations flourish and others don't, how some denominations grow stronger relationships with local churches and others don't, how some church schools drift away from church identity and others continue a close or even strengthened tie to their church. They notice these differences, but they do not immediately become all that interested. Slowly, it seems, they become interested and begin to look at the innovation being proposed that either furthers the existing change or proposes an alternative one. In PMC we look to develop over the first 18 to 24 months a growing percentage of persons interested in the innovation of missional church.

EVALUATION

Once I have become aware of the siren and interested in its meaning, I begin to evaluate possible innovations to respond to the

situation. I have several options and they change given my circumstances and how close the storm is. The set of possibilities is limited
and fairly common.

During this stage of cultural change in a church, the innovation
being proposed will be evaluated and put against other options.
Congregations and their support systems need to evaluate various
possibilities, including those being proposed for a missional church.

TRIAL

Once I have evaluated my options for responding to the air raid
siren, I try out at least one option. Similarly, in the diffusion of innovation in a culture, people try out different options and see how it
goes. Usually it is best to try out options that respond to the breadth
and depth of the cultural change but do not try to change the entire
system at once. A successful diffusion of innovation usually involves
trials that require truly adaptive rather than technical change but only
take on part of the full system of the congregation and the culture that
supports it. This trial part of PMC allows those who want to make
some quick changes to get moving on something, but it also helps
them do something in a manner that moves beyond simply techni-
cally improving their present way of doing things and toward truly
addressing the depth of the cultural change needed to lead to a missional church.

ADOPTION

Once an innovation is tried, and even when some of its trials fail,
a period of adoption usually follows. The innovation becomes a part
of the deep values of the culture, and the congregation begins to carry
on its usual business according to the innovation. This adoptive stage
frees the congregation to make relatively quick changes in many parts
of the congregation's life and in the systems that support it. Once the
missional church innovation is adopted, social and organizational

changes proceed much more quickly and are apparent to most of the people.

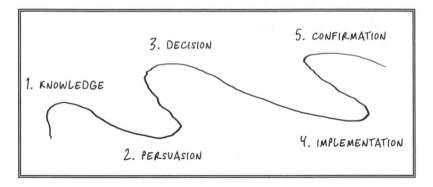

FIVE STAGES OF DECISION MAKING

Everett Rogers not only names the five stages of response to a change; he also delineates five stages of decision making in his model of diffusing innovation in a culture. The stages even fit along the same curve. Awareness moves to interest through knowledge and understanding of a new thing. Interest moves to evaluation through a process of persuasion, either a favorable or unfavorable attitude toward the new thing. The stage of persuasion makes possible the decision to try out some things and experiment with possibilities within the new innovation. The decision for trial of some new ideas, to try out some new practices, some new ways of doing church, ways that reflect a new basic understanding of the culture of congregation, follows. It leads to a period of implementation. Implementation usually requires some strategic planning and reorganization of the congregation on the basis of the new innovation and the experience of the trial practices. Implementation leads to either the confirmation of the new innovation or the rejection of it. When the new innovation is confirmed, the innovation has been diffused and translated into a new moment of the culture of the congregation; it has been adopted.

PEOPLE'S OPENNESS TO CHANGE

Those who lead learn that people differ substantially in their openness to change. Some individuals may be more or less open to change depending on the change being offered. The diffusion of innovation used by PMC recognizes these variations by identifying five different groups on the diffusion-of-innovation journey: (1) innovators; (2) early adopters; (3) early majority; (4) late majority; (5) laggards.

INNOVATORS

Some people just want change; they feel most comfortable changing. Some people, because of their life circumstances or a particular innovation, look for change. In either case, these are likely to be your innovators. These innovators are the brave who take the risks when the cultural innovation is offered. They get the diffusion started. Be aware, however, that they usually cannot make it happen themselves, and some of them get bored easily and will move to the next innovation before the first one has been engaged successfully.

EARLY ADOPTERS

Early adopters are the people who understand that if they are to stay apace with the realities of cultural change, they need to be ahead of the curve. They do not seek change for change's sake, as some of the brave innovators do, but they take a progressive view of life in general or at least life in the local 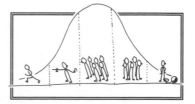 church regarding innovating a missional church.

Be aware that some people who are very progressive in their life outside the church view the local church as the one place that should not change. Indeed, for some of these people, the church's apparent lack of change creates the stability in their lives that makes possible their progressive stance for everything outside the church.

True early adopters have the respect of the majority of the local church's active membership. Precisely because they are respectable, they have significant influence in the congregation. Some consultants call them the influence brokers, and they often are precisely those people who, when convinced, can move much higher percentages of the congregation than the innovators ever could. When I perceive early adopters engaged by missional church, I notice that the entire diffusion of innovation process kicks into a much higher gear. PMC makes these key influence brokers central to the innovation of missional church. In the first 24—36 months, the PMC journey moves from engaging the innovators (2—3 percent of the congregation) to engaging 16—20 percent of the active congregation. Usually once these persons are engaged, the diffusion of innovation is hard to stop; before they are fully engaged, the diffusion of innovation remains highly vulnerable.

EARLY MAJORITY

We have noticed that the early adopters, because they have so much influence, start bringing on an early majority somewhere between 14 and 24 months of the PMC journey. They use their position of respect to reach the thoughtful but not necessarily progressive members of the congregation and engage them in one of the experiments that make up the second phase of PMC. This usually includes engaging persons in the governance structures of the congregation— members of the church council, vestry, session, and so on. The early majority folks are attracted to governance because, as thoughtful persons, they value policy and procedure as necessary actions for the local church's long-term survival. Without engagement of the early majority, the conflicts that cultural change often engenders become extremely divisive for the local church. You will see how the second phase of the PMC journey deliberately assists the innovators and early adopters in engaging the early majority, the thoughtful, and especially those in governance.

LATE MAJORITY

When the first two phases of the PMC journey go well, the momentum picks up and those who have been skeptical about transforming mission begin to see some of the ways that the status quo is broken and also see positive outcomes resulting from the trial period. In the third phase of the PMC journey, Visioning for Embodiment, they get their chance to shape the missional vocation of the congregation and the strategic, long-range plan for walking into God's preferred future. Engaging the late majority, who have taken the "if it ain't broke, don't fix it" stance until now, becomes the point of no return for the diffusion of innovation. As exciting as this moment can be, it also creates a lot of anxiety for the local church system and can create considerable drama just before a plan is adopted and put into action.

LAGGARDS

Every local church has a group of people who simply do not want change—either no change at all or specifically the change brought forth by missional church. Rogers calls those who do not want any change traditional. I prefer to understand them as caught in traditionalism rather than traditional. In PMC we understand tradition as the living faith of the dead and traditionalism as the dead faith of the living.

Quite common in mainline congregations are laggards whom many, including themselves, think of as "tolerant" and "liberal" in their theology and politics. They have become deeply colonized by the modern assumption that "religion is both private and valuable but not public or appropriate for sharing among strangers." They often believe that any missional movement equates to the imposition of

Christian values and beliefs upon those who do not share them. They seem unable to move beyond the virtue of tolerance—clearly preferable to intolerance—to the virtues of appreciation of difference and the freedom to engage in respectful sharing of religious commitments. A congregation has not engaged the depth of the colonization of the church by modernity until it has engaged these deeply held values of modern culture.

PHASES OF THE PARTNERSHIP

We have covered a lot of ground in this chapter. We have contrasted an organizational approach to congregational development and change with one that engages through spiritual discernment the deep values of culture and transforming mission. We have described in a very thin outline the phases of the diffusion of innovation in a culture. We have outlined those phases because they will help you understand the phases of PMC. Each phase of the PMC spiritual journey roughly follows the diffusion of innovation in a culture because, after all, a local church is part of culture. Any model of change that reduces the congregation to either an organization or some mystical communion (even though a local church is both organization and mystical communion) not only fails to understand the depth of change necessary but the nature and nurture of local churches and God's way in this world.

With this all too brief description of the diffusion of innovation, the phases of the PMC journey follow: (1) Discovering; (2) Experimenting; (3) Visioning for Embodiment; and (4) Learning and Growing. Finally, throughout all phases, local churches engage in Sharing and Mentoring. The next five chapters describe this journey.

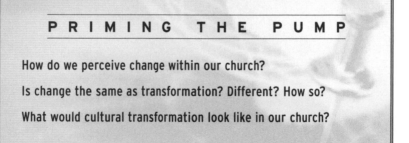

PRIMING THE PUMP

How do we perceive change within our church?

Is change the same as transformation? Different? How so?

What would cultural transformation look like in our church?

CHAPTER 3

PHASE 1: DISCOVERING

LIVING WITHIN THE LIFE OF THE TRINITY

In Partnership for Missional Church™, your local church is invited into a journey of spiritual discernment that engages cultural change and transforms mission.  Theologically speaking, you are being invited into a journey within the life of the living God. For many of you, this seems obvious—you know that you are already in that life. You might be surprised, however, how seldom members of your local church consciously imagine or describe their lives as local church, both gathered and sent, as a journey within the life of the living God.

Indeed, the most frightening discovery we made in our early research in local church renewal was how seldom members of local churches describe their lives in sentences that include God as the subject of action verbs. They almost always describe worship, for example, as something "we do" or "I do." I worship God. I participate in fellowship. We sing hymns and pray. God, in the vast majority of these descriptions gathered by churches' own members and in their own words, is at best the object of human action. Rarely did we hear of God doing something in worship, much less in the community or neighborhood around them.

We discovered that many of the imaginations and descriptions of local church leaders reflect a practical atheism and secularity. Of course, few if any of these same people would say they do not believe that God acts in worship, or in their everyday lives, or in the good works of their local church. No, they always protest when we note how seldom in their stories God is the subject of sentences with action verbs. "We believe God does things," they protest. And of course they 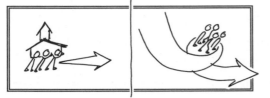 do believe it. They simply don't imagine it as an ordinary part of the way they describe their lives. This is what makes it a practical atheism and secularism rather than one that is held in principle or with intent.

We should not have been surprised by this finding; it reflects the profound shaping of our imaginations by modernity, a modernity that leaves God either as a distant, generic God of nature (sometimes Mother Nature or "The Force") of the deists, or an extremely intimate family God, like "Jesus in our hearts." Where PMC succeeds, it profoundly engages this modern colonization of our imaginations and lives, and it provides safe and wise space and time for imagining God acting in our lives and world, a living God.

In the first phase, and throughout the Partnership journey, we remind local church partners that the living God is triune. Of course, most say, "Yes, God is triune." We have found more often than not, however, that the working theology of PMC partner churches involves a unitarian God. We see how seldom these partners imagine God as a "Being in communion," a Being as communion of Father, Son, and Holy Spirit.

Instead, many imagine God, having created all things, as now observing all things or occasionally intervening in history, but not

always and intimately creating a world. Many yearn for a God, perhaps in contrast to this all-observing distant God, who is close; they may reduce this closeness to Jesus. For them, Jesus is a personal friend and confidant. They do not imagine how the Christian God is always close and distant, stranger and friend, present and absent, hidden and revealed.

If these partners attend to the Spirit at all (and many do not attend to the Spirit at all) they imagine the Holy Spirit as an independent agent who does his/her own thing. Many partners who make much of the works of the Holy Spirit have a hard time relating these works of the Spirit to the ordinary local

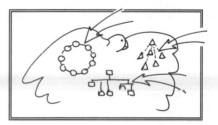

church and the ordinary lives of the congregation's people. They place the Spirit in contrast to the structures of the church, even imagining that the Holy Spirit despises and hates structure and ordering of the church.

In PMC, you are invited to recognize that the Holy Spirit loves structure and form but cannot be contained by any particular structure and form. So the Holy Spirit dwells in and creates many structures and forms but also breaks them open to the release of God's preferred and promised future.

In the first phase of PMC, you discover the most important partner for a missional church: God. Indeed, you will see yourself as created partners, laborers, coworkers in God's mission. Adjusting focus from the church's mission to God's mission massively changes everything. It is God's mission, not the church's. It is God's mission that reflects the very nature and being, movement, and action of God. The very life of God as Father, Son, and Holy Spirit is a process of mission: a Father who sends a Son, a Son who sends a Spirit. In this very likeness of God, we are called, gathered, centered, and sent within the life of the triune God and God's mission, an infinite journey of being called and sent. The activity of finding our place within this journey of the living, triune God, both personally and communally as a local church, is spiritual discernment.

LIVING INTO GOD'S PREFERRED AND PROMISED FUTURE

In PMC, this process of spiritual discernment asks one simple question: What is God's preferred and promised future for our local church? This one question is asked in many and varied ways. To whom and across which barriers is God sending us to be a part of God's mission? What is our local church's missional vocation? How do we

walk into and toward God's preferred and promised future? What are God's gifts in our local church, and how do they relate to what God's mission is in our service area, including the lives of all those we interact with at home, at work, in play, and in friendship? What is God up to in our service area? How can we be a token and sign of that preferred and promised future?

This question about God's preferred and promised future for the local church follows from the nature of the church being shaped by the living, triune God. This connection, while simple, seems ignored in most processes of local church renewal. Indeed, one sees too often an unnecessary conflict arising between competing proposals for renewal. One group of proposals focuses on the future, the new vision. The other proposals focus on the past, faithfulness to the tradition. These two groups see each other as the enemy; what they both share is unquestioning acceptance of the assumptions of modernity and its need for a clean split, a simple either/or. Until advocates of these proposals are able to move beyond these assumptions of modernity, they will remain in hopeless and ineffective struggle with one another rather than walking together into God's preferred future.

Those who focus on faithfulness to the past and tradition profoundly misunderstand the nature of the living, triune God and how faithfulness to this God works with respect to time. This issue of time is something the Greek Orthodox tradition has been trying to talk about to those of us in the Latin West for more than a thousand years,

and we have had a very hard time hearing it. They keep noting how "faithfulness" in the western, Latin-based church always focuses on the past. The Latin West asks, "Are we being faithful to the

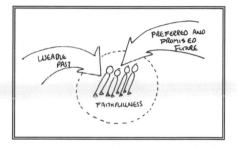

instituting moment of the church in the life of Jesus?" The dominant answer in the Latin West, the Roman Catholic answer, is that we are being faithful because we follow the apostolic succession of those Jesus appointed. Some Protestant or free church traditions of the Latin West pick some other moment of the instituting of the church in the life of Jesus as the test of whether we are being faithful. Most of us of the Latin West say to the Greek Orthodox that faithfulness is about being faithful to the instituting moment of the church in the life of Jesus.

Our Greek Orthodox brothers and sisters reply, "not enough." To be faithful, you must also be faithful to the constituting moment of the church that comes, not from the past, but by the will of the Father, in the person of the Son who will judge us at the end of time, through the power of the Holy Spirit, from God's absolute future. Faithfulness is as much about faithfulness to God's future as it is faithfulness to God's past; our God is a living, triune God who dwells in all times, and in the life of God all times are present; the church participates already but not yet in that once and future life of God. Thus the question of faithfulness is not past vs. future but finding a useable past for our faithfulness to God's preferred and promised future.

One of my mentors, Henry, illustrated his own discovery of this learning to be faithful to both past and future from his experience as a young, white pastor in a very secure, powerful, established, tall-steeple church in Augusta, Georgia, during the time of the civil rights movement. His congregation valued deeply its tradition and sought sincerely to be faithful to God's will and always imagined their faithfulness as faithfulness to the past.

Henry was a student of liturgical renewal, and through that scholarship he discovered the Greeks' critique of the liturgy and doctrine of the church of the Latin West, especially in their rejection of imagining the Mass, the Lord's Supper, the Eucharist, as primarily a reproduction, remembrance, or reenacting of Thursday or Friday of Holy Week. Instead, the Eucharist is primarily the remembrance, anamnesis, of the night of Easter Sunday on the road to Emmaus. Here the church in the person of two confused and discouraged disciples are returning to their everyday lives, the lives between the Resurrection and God's promised future. Here the church is met on the road by a stranger who opens the scriptures to them and is revealed to them as the Risen Lord only when they invite this stranger to join them at table fellowship and ask the stranger to offer the blessing of the bread. In this blessing of the bread, in this hospitality to and of the Stranger, the Risen Lord is revealed to his church, his body.

This table fellowship that is the promised future of God made present, this foretaste of the Messianic banquet, shapes the church's life within the life of the living, triune God. So Henry began to teach, preach, and envision with his fellow members of the body of Christ about who would be at that table fellowship in God's promised future. Would persons of color be there? Might we not start walking with them now into God's promised future? Might we not recognize that we are all depending upon God's hospitality anyway, including and especially in how we gather as his local body? Through such teaching, preaching, and visioning they discerned their missional call, their part of God's mission in their community, their next steps into God's preferred and promised future, by embodying their lives and ministries across the boundary of race.

In contrast to the traditionalist focus on faithfulness to the past, the other dominant proposals in contemporary approaches to church renewal focus almost exclusively upon the future, too often to the exclusion or trivialization of the past. These processes, borrowed from often outdated models of business visioning and planning, born in modernity and reflecting its profound control of the imagination of the church in Christendom, imagine a relatively small group of people casting a vision and getting the rest to "own it" or "buy in" to their vision. Or others, in marked contrast to this utilitarian top-down approach to visioning, propose an egalitarian, bottom-up approach in which all persons are invited to express their vision for the local church and together create a shared communal vision.

In both the utilitarian top-down and the expressivity bottom-up approaches, the convictions are that the future is in our hands (either the top or the bottom) and that it is a matter of the future alone, the one we imagine and envision. We are the chief actors. We have no need of the past; indeed, tradition in these models usually is ignored or even denigrated as the problem to be overcome. These models have all the strengths and weaknesses of modernity and, like the gap model into which they too often feed, they imagine the church without the richness of tradition, the democracy of the dead, the living faith of the dead and, frankly, a very foreshortened sense of the future.

Nonetheless, these future-focused models clearly represent a step forward from the dominant realities of all too many local churches. In most of our research, we find that most local churches have little or no sense of their future or of God's claim on that future. Indeed, most do not imagine that God cares enough about their particular local church or the people within its service area to have a preferred future into which God is calling and sending them. In thousands of interviews gathered in their own language by their own members, local churches revealed that they have little or no sense of their future as anything but a continuation of their present. They surely do not imagine God calling and sending them into a specific future.

In the end, the evidence is overwhelming: there is a deep spiritual crisis revealed in the imaginations and hearts of these people's stories about their own lives and about their local church. They have practical atheist, secular imaginations caught in the present with very little past and very little future. PMC addresses this deep spiritual crisis of the imagination and heart by dwelling in the Word of God.

DWELLING IN THE WORD

On the basis of more than 17 years of research on how the Bible actually functions in local churches (as opposed to the doctrinal claims made for it by those local churches' members or leaders), we have found disturbing realities amounting to a crisis. Even local churches that make much of their commitment to the Bible as the Word of God more often than not suffer from biblical illiteracy.

More significantly, they illustrate from their own stories that they do not have biblical imaginations, imaginations that grow out of Scripture.

Of course they use the Bible. They may use the Bible like some tool with which they accomplish their own purposes and ends, but seldom do they demonstrate the capacity to imagine their everyday lives within the narrative of Scripture. Indeed, their focus on the Bible is strangely unrelated to this living within and out of the world in front of the biblical text. This disturbing reality led Church Innovations to work on models of allowing the Word of God to use us rather than our using it; or, more biblically speaking, for our dwelling within the Word.

Easier said than done, I assure you. Indeed, we at Church Innovations believe our most significant innovation in our nearly two decades of "innovating your church's capacities to be renewed in mission" is the various ways we have innovated the capacity of churches to dwell in the Word of God.

PMC begins with a text that was given to us through our work with our partners: Luke 10:1-12. This text came to Church Innovations through a planning weekend with the Minnesota Council on Indian Work of the Episcopal Diocese of Minnesota. On the first weekend of September 1995, we joined their leadership in a retreat at the Episcopal House of Prayer on the campus of the Benedictine community and St. John's University in Collegeville, Minnesota. We spent the entire weekend dwelling in this text, chosen because it was assigned for the first day of our retreat as part of the celebration of David Oakerhater, an early Episcopal Native American evangelist and missionary. In the process of dwelling in this Word we carried on all of our planning for our shared work. After the weekend, Church Innovations staff returned with the text to our next staff meeting and began the tradition of dwelling in this Word whenever the staff or the Board of Directors gathers.

Out of these ongoing experiences of Dwelling, we integrated all of our work at Church Innovations and developed and formed the next stages of PMC within this Word. If you look back over the last couple of chapters and then read Luke 10:1-12, it should be relatively clear to you how profoundly this passage shapes the imagination of PMC. We are sent in pairs; partnering is essential. We depend upon the hospitality of those to whom we are sent. Present in the text are all persons of the Trinity, the sense of partnering, being called, and being sent to places where Jesus has not yet gone but that God has created and where the Holy Spirit creates the peace of welcome despite Jesus' absence. The harvest is the Lord's, not ours, and the reign of God is near no matter how the potential hosts respond. So much more can be said to show how PMC grows out of dwelling in the Word of God.

In each of the meetings of each of the phases of PMC, in ever increasing numbers, places, and times, local churches leaders will invite people to dwell in the Word. Over time, the attitudes and beliefs, minimum knowledge base, skills, and enduring habits of Dwelling in the Word form and reform the local church. Within this spiritual practice of Dwelling in the Word, the other practices of spiritual discernment grow and are fed.

In Dwelling in the Word, the same Word over long periods of time and diverse moments and spaces in the process of spiritual discernment, something close to a miracle happens to the imaginations and hearts and eventually the actions of the leaders of the local church and of the many who follow them. They begin to imagine their lives being lived within the life the living, triune God. Within this imagination, they experience both the at-hand-ness of the Reign of God and also its clear not-in-hand-ness. At hand, yes. In hand, no.

Leaders and those who follow them begin to speak freely of their sense of God's engagement in their lives and a sense of their partnership within the mission of God. Within this strengthened Christian imagination, they begin to see and experience the world, especially their immediate community, service area, and those with whom they live their daily lives, in new terms, no longer only as humans would see them but also as God does.

DISCOVERING CONGREGATIONAL LEADERS

Each phase of PMC develops leaders. Through two decades of leadership studies, Church Innovations has come to understand leadership as much a matter of time as a matter of space or position in the structure. If a leader does not have time for process, he or she cannot truly lead but rather ends up reacting to the challenges of the local church. Of course, part of leadership requires responding to immediate challenges and managing them, but true leadership depends on having the time and ability to define the challenge (rather than simply respond to it) within the vision and plan of action based on God's preferred and promised future. This requires growing leadership out of a process of spiritual discernment about the local church's missional vocation. So leadership development and PMC go well together.

From the beginning of Phase 1, we discover leaders by helping those who come forward and those we seek out as partners to move deeply into the process of spiritual discernment. The first group of leaders includes the staff of the local church, whether full-time or not. Those who have the public responsibility for the primary care and nurture of the local church are staff, whether teaching, preaching, ruling, governing, presiding, singing, directing, and so forth. Within this leadership group some may discern a clearer calling to this work of PMC than others, but all become a part of the process.

In the early years of PMC, through our process of a bimonthly phone loop, we discovered that most of the leaders with public responsibility did not have the personal spiritual practices to maintain a focus upon God's preferred and promised future in their own lives, much less the life of the local church. For example, more often than not, they spent most of their time with Scripture using it to accomplish their work. They studied Scripture to preach or teach or perform some other leader function. Scripture was reduced to a tool for ministry rather than the Word of God in which they dwelled. Further, they had never learned or did not engage in the practice of prayer and meditation. They allowed their lives to be cluttered with an overwhelming sense of many things to do.

Of course, any leader has many things to do, more than likely many good things to do. As St. Augustine wisely notes in the Confessions, God blesses us with many good things to love and good things to do, indeed, more good things to love and to do than we are able to do and love well. We are mightily tempted, indeed driven, to try to do them all, or at least many more of them than we can do and love well. We dissipate our lives into nothing, and, like cold water onto a hot griddle, our love and action evaporate into thin air if we do not order our loving by God's will.

As any time management specialist will tell you, the secret is in short lists created within appropriate priorities. Too many of us have long lists that have not been put through the practice of setting priorities. Augustine's short list is simple: love God and do what you will. Ah, so simple a statement and so true, but the spiritual practice of discerning God's will for us and for our community is essential to create the short list and to focus on it. If the public leaders of the congregation do not have this spiritual practice in their lives, they are very unlikely to provide the leadership necessary to focus on the local church's missional vocation. Instead, they will dissipate their lives and the lives of the congregation into nothingness. We have heard the steam rising into thin air in phone loop sessions where a staff person from Church Innovations prays with leaders and they talk about how things are going. More often than not the leader either consciously or unconsciously sounds like cold water hitting a scalding hot griddle.

As a result, we put into place a deliberate process of gathering these public leaders the day before or after each of the three cluster events in each phase to help them focus and reflect on the spiritual practices suitable to public leadership in the local church. These sessions work on the attitudes and beliefs, skills, knowledge base, and habits of spiritual discernment. Each leader discovers a partner for the work of innovating spiritual practices. They establish over time their personal habits and practices and encourage one another in developing them.

While this personal work goes on in these public leaders' lives, they must also discern who will make up the PMC Steering Team, a group of 5-7 people with very different gifts and callings. At least one, hopefully more, must be able to catch a vision and pass it on. At least one must be able to crunch numbers and assist the team and the congregation in narrating those numbers with the biblical narrative and the emerging sense of missional vocation. At least one must be gifted at attending to the relationships within the group and building a strong sense of team. Another needs to be an influence broker within the larger congregation and understand the real power and decision-making processes. Last but not least, one must have the gift of prayer, the ability to invite the group to prayer and Dwelling in the Word.

Of all the leaders developed in the Partnership process, the PMC Steering Team commits to the greatest amount of work (roughly one 90-minute meeting a month and another 90 minutes of personal work time) and the longest period of time. They guide the first 14-18 months, including Phases 1 and 2. From month 12 forward they begin to hand on their leadership to different individuals whom they invite and develop as the next generation of Steering Team, also a 14-18 month commitment.

The Steering Team leads the local church's organizations, commit-tees, and social groups in Dwelling in the Word, and guides all the logistics of the process while keeping the end of the process in sight. The team integrates PMC into the governance processes of the local church throughout the first 14 months. Team members are responsi-ble for engaging the governance of the congregation in Dwelling in the Word, in the reports generated by other teams, and in the narra-tion of the numbers and stories gathered from the wider immediate community. In the last months of the Discovering Phase, they will bring the governing board, session, council, vestry, and so on into Phase 2, Experimenting. In all of this work, the Steering Team and staff tell the story of the congregation's past, assist the congregation in finding a useable future within that past, bring to the congrega-tion's attention the partners they are discovering, and keep the focus on the discernment of a missional vocation.

DWELLING IN THE WORLD

An amazing miracle follows as the Steering Team leads the local church in Dwelling in the Word together over a significant period of time: leaders and active members begin to experience their everyday lives and the community into which Jesus sends them in a new way. Before the practices and habits of Dwelling in the Word are well in place, many if not most local church leaders experience the changes and forces at work in their communities as primarily the work of prin-cipalities and powers not to be trusted and up to little or no good. Indeed, to use a sharp and perhaps offensive expression, they tend to ask, "What in the name of hell is going on here?" When the habit of Dwelling in the Word is in place they tend to ask, "What in heaven's name is going on here? What is God up to here in this place and time, in the relationships both within and without the local church?"

Within the questions formed and shaped by Dwelling in the Word, it is possible to begin to examine a number of aspects of the local church within its immediate world. One of these aspects involves the demographics and psychographics of the congregation, its immediate environment, and the people God may be sending the local church to join in mission. Many processes of visioning and planning draw upon demographics and the subfield of psychographics. They draw from census data that tells many things about the individuals and households within a community, including race, gender, income level, tenure in their present home, level of education, and type of household. Similar information regarding reli-

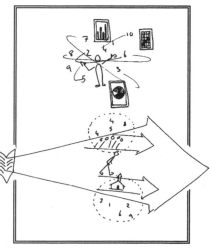

gious preference, buying patterns, psychological types, and opinions is available from other sources. Beyond a shadow of doubt these sources of information represent real knowledge and facts about the immediate environment and world of the local church. Very few if any models of planning and visioning, however, know how to make these facts into information that is useable. More importantly, very few models of planning and visioning understand the real dangers of continuing a very bad moral habit of modernity reinforced by the kind of knowledge and facts available in such data: the objectification of persons and communities.

Attending a client conference of a state-of-the-art provider of demographic and psychographic data, our staff was astounded to discover how few, if any, of the clients knew how to help local churches make sense of this data or move beyond the objectification of persons and households that these materials encourage and facilitate. We even met two client representatives who held doctoral degrees in sociology who admitted that they found it extremely difficult to avoid these pitfalls when working with local churches. Of course, the quality of the reports, both printed and online, was impressive, giving the judicatory officials using these reports the impression of an overwhelming sense of knowledge. This knowledge, however, objectified people and communities and prevented relational ministry.

We decided to study in depth a few judicatory leaders who used these products to see how well they worked with local churches. Even in the few cases where these leaders understood the process and materials well, it was rare indeed to find local church leaders able to engage this material in the powerful ways necessary to redevelop local churches and innovate missional church.

What was missing was not more sociological sophistication—indeed, this was not that important for those who were able to use the material well—but the ability to narrate the numbers. Human beings understand "facts" and engage knowledge within a narrative. Local churches that want to innovate missional church need to understand demographic and psychological facts within the Christian narrative and be able to imagine real persons, not objectified abstractions, within their sense of what God is up to within their lives.

The process of Dwelling in the Word frames the narration of the numbers. Within the biblical narrative, the local church can listen to its own stories and the stories of people in its service area. Through a process we call Congregational Discovery, developed by Dr. Patricia Taylor Ellison and myself, we use applied ethnography to gather these narratives and to narrate these numbers. Applied ethnography, a well-established model of social scientific research, allows people within the local church and within their service area to explore open-ended questions in their own language and tell their own stories.

Who are the key persons in this Congregational Discovery process? Listening Leaders. They are persons selected from the congregation who, more often than not, have not been perceived as leaders at all. These are persons who have the gift of listening people into free speech and recording with clarity, accuracy, and succinctness what individuals and groups say in answer to the open-ended questions. During the first phase of PMC, these Listening Leaders profoundly shape the discoveries that are made. They are trained to carry on the discovery process, developing questions appropriate to their own local culture and conducting interviews while protecting anonymity. Completed interviews are sent to Church Innovations, where teams of readers analyze and interpret these answers and stories through diverse lenses appropriate for innovating a missional church. A reading team report is returned to the Listening Leaders, who, together with other leaders, including the Steering Team, disseminate the findings to the local church.

Through these steps, Listening Leaders and members of the Steering Team examine the various connections between the individuals, households, and informal and formal organizations of the local church and members of the community and its organizations.

The image below illustrates in a simplified form three social groups to whom we want to listen. They are placed within three concentric circles starting with the smallest in the center containing the family.

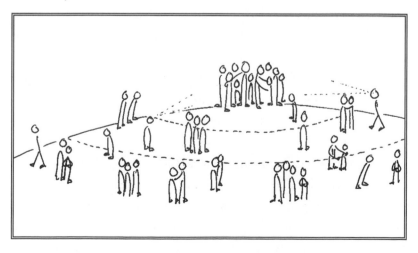

The family, a group of persons, whether formal leaders or not, communicate with one another, recruit one another to get things done, and informally decide what gets done in the local church. The family can be as large as 60 persons but usually is considerably smaller.

The second concentric circle, usually much larger in number than the family, is the inside strangers. These persons might have been part of the family at one time but no longer participate in the informal system of communicating and decision-making. They often attend regularly but generally "watch" church and allow the family to decide most matters.

The third concentric circle is the outside strangers. These are the persons who, when they enter the gathered community, are clearly outsiders. They know, the other two groups know, everybody knows they don't belong. It may be their manner of dress, speech, language, or other behaviors. They may be related to members of the congregation or not. They may be active in some program the congregation sponsors or belong to a group that uses the church building but is not related to the life of the local church.

While each of these groups can meaningfully be understood in more complex ways, this fairly simple model approaches different groups for understanding the congregation's culture and those it seeks to serve.

In this process, the church's ties to civil society are explored. Civil society is that part of our community that carries on our shared purposes and interests, that depends primarily on neither government nor business nor upon intimate and familial ties. Some congregations understand themselves to be a critical part of civil society; others hardly notice it. Within the process of innovating a missional church, local church leaders are invited to discover the congregation's role as public companions within this civil society. Some very powerful discoveries about connecting the life of the local church to the mission of God come from exploring this role of public companion and the dynamics of civil society.

The numbers gathered in demographic surveys become part of (1) the biblical narrative, (2) the narrative of the local church, (3) the local church's role as public moral companion within civil society, and (4) the narratives of real, specific persons and households within the service area of the local church. As these narratives engage one another, edges and conflicts, challenges and opportunities, failures and achievements of the mission of God take shape in the imaginations and hearts of the leaders of the local church and leaders within the community it serves.

DISCOVERING OTHER CONGREGATIONS

Over the years, we have learned that congregations have the potential to learn more from one another than they could from us. We have also learned that for one reason or another they couldn't learn from one another or didn't try to learn from one another. How often has your congregation established a deliberate process for learning from another congregation? Not very often, I would guess, if you are like most of the congrega- 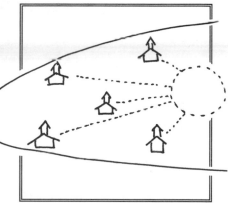 tions with whom we have worked over these last two decades.

To learn from one another, congregations need to be brokered to one another. This is a critical insight to PMC. PMC uses the local judicatory and Church Innovations to broker congregations to one another. We place the congregations into a process of spiritual discernment with one another that helps them discover other congregations as partners for missional church.

Initially this brokering involves helping the public leaders of these congregations develop a sense of shared purpose and trust with one another so that they can begin to learn from one another. From the beginning, even before the first cluster meetings, this work of community building begins. In the months prior to the first cluster meetings, the public leaders of the congregations begin to develop plans and habits for partnering together. The day before the first cluster meeting, these public leaders spend time in prayer together, working on the spiritual practices necessary to carry out their place in the process of spiritual discernment that is PMC.

SYSTEMS THAT SUPPORT INNOVATING MISSIONAL CHURCH

We learn the hard way too often at Church Innovations. For years we worked either with individual congregations or with clusters of congregations. When we could, we received the blessing of judicatory leaders but, more often than not, we did not develop those relationships into partnerships. After some 15 years of doing this work, enjoying at best the nodding acceptance of our working with clusters of congregations, we evaluated our long-term effectiveness and found that, without full partnership with judicatory staff, our chances of sustained innovation of missional church were greatly reduced. We even uncovered substantial, sustained effort on the part of judicatory and churchwide staff to undercut those places where a growing movement was in place.

Here we discovered a painful fact about many mainline churchwide staffs: they feel extremely vulnerable to the rapid ongoing transformation of denominational systems in this New Missional Era. They spend very large amounts of their time reacting to this profound transformation and likely, without considerable effort on our part, perceive our work as competition with theirs. They pass this perception on to their mid-governing body leaders who, to show loyalty in this time of high stress and transformation, act on this perception. Time and time again, we found former staff at churchwide and judicatory level admitting to deliberately seeking to undercut the introduction of missional church.

We at Church Innovations and the Gospel and Our Culture Network, based mostly in the academy of the church, failed to understand these pressures and became defensive in the face of the churchwide perception of our work. We were strongly based in theory and comfortable with the language of social scientific and theological research, but we often failed to develop genuine partnership with judicatory and churchwide staffs. We also made mistakes with congregations that created more work for already-burdened judicatory staffs. Without partnership, these mistakes on our part became the opportunity to undercut our long-term purpose.

We commissioned a longevity study of our work and found that one of the major changes we needed to put into place was creating partnerships with judicatory leadership and, where possible, with churchwide staff. We also found that, because of our strong academic and research credentials, we could bring the academy into the work of PMC: researchers and schools of theology that are dedicated to innovating a missional church. In the last seven years we have developed strong interdependent partnerships with some 30 seminaries around the world, other institutes and research organizations like ourselves, dozens of denominations, and hundreds of judicatory staffs in these denominations. We have studied these systems using concepts of systems theory and have gained tremendous insight into their ability to support innovating missional church.

This chapter has described Phase 1 of PMC. The focus has been on discovering, discovering through listening. Through listening, a growing circle of leaders discover God, others within their congregation and community, and other congregations as partners for a missional church. The next chapter describes Phase 2. This phase focuses on experimenting, experimenting with change that engages deep, cultural transformation.

PRIMING THE PUMP

In our congregation's experience, what does it mean to "live within the life of the Trinity"?

Is it an intentional way of life? a basic orientation we don't have to think about?

To what extent do we invite the Triune God to lead us—personally, individually, communally?

What are the stories that point to our experience of living within the life of the Trinity?

CHAPTER 4

PHASE 2: EXPERIMENTING

TO REVIEW, THE PURPOSE of this book is to describe a journey of spiritual discernment that is done communally within local congregations, among 12-16 partner churches, and with still other partners. I have underlined the importance of exploring innovations primarily within the culture of the local church rather than primarily within its organizational structures. Without exploring innovation within the culture of the local church, the congregation runs the risk of being ineffective, inefficient, and unfaithful, in short, limiting itself to organizational change. The result, more often than not, is greater harm rather than help in engaging the local church community in the New Missional Era.

Chapter 2 addressed the distinction between cultural and organizational change with worship, small group, and conflict resolution examples. We borrowed from established theories of cultural change to get some sense of how it takes place and how we might expect to engage the culture in our process of spiritual discernment. You will recall that the first part of cultural change 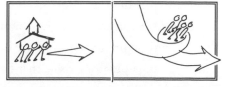 focuses on awareness, a growing sense that change is necessary. Chapter 3 outlined the process of listening that allows for discovering partners in this journey.

The PMC journey so far is designed to capture the imaginations and actions of your brave innovators and some of your early adopters. Now we turn to capturing the imagination and actions of your thoughtful, progressive leaders who get things done and those who guide and govern the congregation over significant periods of time.

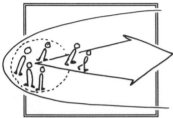

This chapter describes experimenting as a way of engaging these groups of people to relate the gospel, the local church, and its culture. Rather than take on the whole system of the local church, this phase of our spiritual journey asks and teaches leaders to experiment on one or two pieces of local church life and work as they encounter those whom they believe God is calling them to engage in mission. These one or two pieces need to touch the entire

system in innovation but do not attempt to change the entire system. Finding and working on these pieces of the system challenges leaders to explore adaptive rather than technical change, a distinction to which I'll return. However, first I want to explain how we came to this Experimenting Phase.

HARD LESSONS: BEYOND GRAND PLANS TO EXPERIMENTING

The Experimenting Phase grew out of hard lessons over the past 17 years. Our current Phase 3, Visioning for Embodiment, began as Phase 2 in the spiritual journey. We borrowed from visioning models and long-range planning tools that had served well in other settings. Time and time again, however, two of the cluster gatherings in Phase 2 revealed significant obstacles in almost every congregation. Indeed, this pattern became so common that our staff renamed these two cluster meetings "hitting the wall."

Congregational leaders described how they kept hitting a wall of obstacles to forming a useable plan of action. Of course, obstacles are common in planning processes. We understood this pattern and also borrowed from well-established techniques for counteracting obstacles. In those cluster gatherings we taught ways of naming obstacles and discovering paths around or over those obstacles.

While these techniques often worked, they did not address a major dynamic of the spiritual journey in the vast majority of local churches: the polarity between early victories and long-term change. Further, these techniques did not effectively, efficiently, and faithfully attend to the political realities of people who need quick success to be motivated to action versus those who are suspicious of quick success. Let's explore both dynamics.

EARLY VICTORIES & LONG-TERM CHANGE

One of the basic challenges of this spiritual journey is the polarity between the understandable need for some early victories and the painful fact that we are working for long-term, even multiple-generational change. Many of the local churches that join PMC have been busy adapting themselves to death. They have 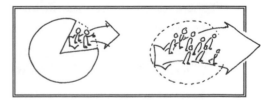 either allowed the profound changes in their immediate environment to go unnoticed or spent most of their time in culture critique and complaint. They notice that they are losing active members; they see that regular worshipers are growing older; they become proficient at blaming the culture around them, or the people who leave, or the younger generations.

Now, as they join PMC, some among them are looking for a quick fix, some magic formula that, if applied, can respond to this massive change in their immediate environment and the culture that supports it. Others are equally suspicious of such quick fixes. Their life experience has taught them quick fixes rapidly become passing fads. Worse, they believe that quick fixes trivialize what really counts about Christian community.

Incidentally, we have seen pastors/ministers become very sophisticated at avoiding both options by becoming armchair critics. Their sermons begin to show an increasing analysis of the wrongs of the culture, even the culture of the local church. If, for example, the local church is in an urban neighborhood where new immigrants have replaced the settled community, the pastor/minister might well become a critic of the congregation's racism and classism, of suburban flight, or of the individualist religion of the United States. The list can go on and does. The crux of this situation is that the pastor/minister, no matter how sophisticated, becomes a culture critic instead of someone who leads a spiritual journey to missional church.

Time and time again, as a systematic theologian—a calling given to being an armchair critic—I have noticed how my best students often fail to be effective, efficient, and faithful leaders because I taught them how to do the critique but not how to provide theological and spiritual leadership. In contrast, I have seen my B students take the same lessons of theological critique and place them within a sense of spiritual leadership by forming community with this new environment, joining it to the central spiritual energies and witness of their tradition and the local church they serve. What a contrast!

These effective spiritual leaders have been able to take the need for quick fixes and tie this energy to long-term change. They, too, need some early victories. They are open to trying new things but also  realize that the new things must engage the deep cultural values of the local church they serve, lest they prove a passing fad or create unnecessary and dysfunctional conflict. So they encourage experimentation, new ways of forming Christian community that match the people within their service group with those whom they believe God is calling them to serve. These leaders understand the polarity between the need for some early victories and the enduring multiple-generational change necessary, and they manage this dynamic well. And they must. Here's why.

SPRINTERS & LONG-DISTANCE RUNNERS

Attempts to bring forth change reveal two very different groups within a congregation: (1) those who need to see some immediate success and change in the life of the local church and (2) those who understand that this kind of change requires long-term, deep, cultural engagement that seldom produces or is even helped by quick fixes. These two groups of people often see each other as the enemy. When they do, they can sustain long-term conflict that prevents significant fulfillment of either of their desires. However, they might see each other as two very different but important elements of the community. As one pastor who had learned to manage this polarity well explained to me, one group was made up of sprinters and the other of long-distance runners. When he wanted change, he would ask the governance board of the local church (the long-distance runners) to give permission for a small "task force" of persons who were creative and wanted change in a certain critical part of the church's life (the sprinters). The task force of sprinters would not work on anything that did not bring about change in a few months or so. As long as their leadership would stay in touch with the leadership of the governance board through the entire process, the two 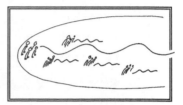 played well with each other, and major change was initiated in the local church.

I asked this pastor what role he had played. Had he chaired the governance board or the task force? "No," he said with a look of dismay at the stupidity of my questions. "I was the secretary of the  task force. I reminded them of what they had decided the last time and what they would do the next time. I interpreted for both leadership groups what each was saying and doing." I was quite impressed to watch this senior pastor, who had taken this congregation through massive change over 21 years, effectively use his skills as an interpreter of Scripture and of the words and actions of both sprinters and long-distance runners to weave a narrative that included them both within God's mission. He listened well, he interpreted well, and he helped them clarify their witness and mission well. All the while he was their secretary.

TECHNICAL AND ADAPTIVE CHANGE

Whether instinctively or with reflective understanding, effective leaders are able to see that the kind of change they need to experiment with is about deep patterns of life and ministry in the local church culture rather than something they already know how to do, simply applying their existing competencies to do it. They understand the difference between adaptive (deep engagement with the entire system) and technical (using existing competencies to solve an easily identified "problem") change.

Technical change dominates all the quick fixes offered: 8 characteristics, 44 ways to increase worship attendance, 4 ways to improve giving, 8 patterns of spiritual discernment. If you can give people a number of things to do and assume they know how to do them, and those things will solve the "problem," this is by definition a technical change. Technical change models are essential to our everyday lives;

they make up the majority of the change we must engage in from day to day.

Recently I was on a flight from Europe seated next to an executive of the airline I was flying. He and I were talking about the challenges facing this airline, which had recently filed for bankruptcy. Many of the challenges required technical change, things they knew how to do and simply were not doing as efficiently and effectively 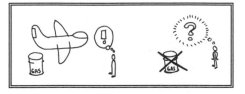 as they might. He noted, however, that the underlying problems within the airline industry would require deeper, adaptive change that no one in the industry could do at that moment. For example, he said, "This industry depends upon petroleum, an increasingly limited, volatile-in-price commodity. We need to find alternative solutions to providing air travel." There are limits to making planes more efficient and effective (technical change); we need to innovate a mode of air travel that does not depend on petroleum. Right now we don't have an answer to this challenge, and it probably requires serious cultural change. Experience tells us, however, such deep change is possible and even likely. Adaptive change happens in all cultures that thrive.

Congregations need both kinds of change, but in this phase of the PMC spiritual journey, we invite small groups of people in task forces called Missional Engagement Teams to take on a small piece of the congregation's practices that relates to the entire system and tackle an adaptive change. These groups will work with the governance board so that those who govern long-  term change are engaged with those who seek short-term action. Of course, there will be tension between these two groups and even within them. Part of a healthy system that innovates missional church is the real conflict that generates the energy for the innovation.

Those who see the deep, long-term, even multigenerational task that lies before them might be tempted to take on the whole system at once. They may allow the depth and breadth of the challenge to convince them that from the first minute they must take on every part of the congregation's life and ministry if they are to be a part of God's innovating missional church. Our experience with this total system approach has usually been unhappy, dysfunctional, and ineffective conflict. The realists among this group become overwhelmed with all the obstacles they can name; they often throw their hands up in discouragement or disgust after a couple attempts at taking on the whole system.

Those who desire early victories may want to ignore the need for adaptive change. Missional Engagement Teams take on both early victories and adaptive change. A Missional Engagement Team takes on an adaptive challenge that is related to the entire system, but is small enough that the experiment can fail without threatening the whole. This is the critical point: This is a limited experiment! A trial period! It is fine to fail! It may even be a necessary part of the journey of spiritual discernment to fail!

This willingness to experiment, try out, even to fail challenges is an uncommon characteristic in most PMC congregations. They have seldom if ever given themselves permission to experiment and fail. They may fail, to be sure, but they immediately sweep the failure under the rug.

This pattern of sweeping failure under the rug kills more often than it gives life. Innovation requires experimentation; experimentation involves more failure than success; if you do not examine the failure, reflect upon it, and learn from it, you increase the chance that in the not-too-distant future you will repeat the failure. We call this process of learning from failure and mistakes *excellent failure* or *excellent mis-*

takes. Excellent failure and excellent mistakes are those we reflect upon and learn from.

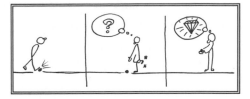

Most congregations are risk averse, and they function within a church structure that is risk averse. Somehow, Christian community within the Christendom establishment learned these deep messages: Do not experiment with forming Christian community! Do not change anything important! Above all, do not fail! And, if you fail, sweep it under the rug.

Perhaps this cultural pattern supports one of the most substantial adaptive challenges for your congregation. The very thought of experimenting, of trying something that is likely to fail, especially if the experiment involves an important aspect of the culture, simply is unacceptable. Your congregation might consider such experimentation unfaithful or trivializing.

CHANGE AS
LISTS OF THINGS TO DO

CHANGE AS A
JOURNEY OF DISCOVERY

It might not leave room for failure. If so, your congregation is like most we know.

Of course, what does it mean when we so fail to trust God's promises to the church that we cannot try something new? What does it mean when we are a community that so distrusts God's mercy among us that we cannot risk failure? What does it mean when we have created such a risk-averse culture that we will adapt ourselves to death rather than trust God's preferred and promised future? Clearly one of the deep adaptive challenges the congregation is likely to face in this phase of the PMC spiritual journey is the contrast between trusting God's promises of mercy and a future and our guaranteeing failure by failing to risk.

At this point in the journey, both sprinters and long-distance runners share the same spiritual crisis. Both need to take on an adaptive challenge that engages the entire system without changing the whole system. Both need to find some change in practice that they know they do not know how to do. Both are asked to trust God's promise of mercy when they fail and to trust God's promise of a future for God's people, even if not for their particular local church.

By authorizing Missional Engagement Teams, the long-distance runners say, "It is okay to experiment on an adaptive challenge, and we will create a safe environment for trial and error. We will support these sprinters in the face of likely criticism and condemnation for failure." The sprinters, by accepting this authorization and challenge to be on a Missional Engagement Team, admit that they do not already know the answer; indeed, they probably don't even know the adaptive challenge they face. They will forego the quick fix and enter a really risky experimentation that leads to a challenge to the entire system, putting into place a real change of practice.

When such persons join together in mutual support and aid, the PMC journey gets hotter and more vibrant; it begins to cook. Now, as never before, it is important to remember that this journey of spiritual discernment takes place by the will of God in the person of Jesus and by the power of the Holy Spirit. It is a process of spiritual discernment within the life of the Trinity.

ACTING AND REFLECTING

As mentioned in earlier chapters, this spiritual journey engages an ever-growing percentage of the congregation's leaders in acting and reflecting. Each cluster gathering invites this increasing circle of leaders to reflect upon what they have done. Such reflection takes place within the narrative of Scripture, through Dwelling in the Word, listening one another into free speech within that Word of God, praying together, attending to God's continuing presence, and listening for God's preferred and promised future. Each cluster gathering instructs this circle of leaders to do some things between one cluster gathering and the next. During this second phase, the governance board and Missional Engagement Team are taught how to

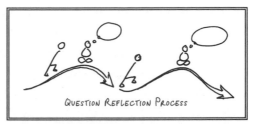

QUESTION REFLECTION PROCESS

take an already-identified adaptive challenge and clarify it into more specific questions. They are taught how to explore the adaptive challenge, to which they do not have answers, and create an experiment that engages the clarified adaptive challenge within the entire system of the congregation without changing the entire system. At each cluster gathering, the Steering Team, governance board, and Missional Engagement Team will reflect upon what they have done and prepare to act again.

There will be people who consider such obvious political and practical engagement in change and innovation very unspiritual. They have accepted the modern dogma that the spiritual is intimate, otherworldly, impractical, and unpolitical, and will often be scandalized by such a mundane spirituality.

Similarly, some so-called "practical leaders" will find spending time Dwelling in the Word, listening one another into free speech within the Word, holding themselves open to God's preferred and promised future by way of extended prayer, and conversing with God a waste of time. They may tolerate these actions as a necessary part of church, but as the process heats up, they will be tempted to set these spiritual practices aside as impractical or something others can do for them. They will be tempted to say, "As practical leaders, persons who do the 'business' of the congregation, we need to put our focus on new decisions and let those who have the gift of prayer do their work."

Without denying that different gifts need to be deployed at different places and times, it is extremely dangerous to ever lose a sense of forming Christian community in Dwelling in the Word, listening one another into free speech, and holding the community open to God's preferred and promised future through prayer and praise. Acting and reflecting, struggling and fighting, failing and forgiving within the Word of God reflects and is shaped by the life of the Trinity; it is spiritual discernment within the life of the Trinity.

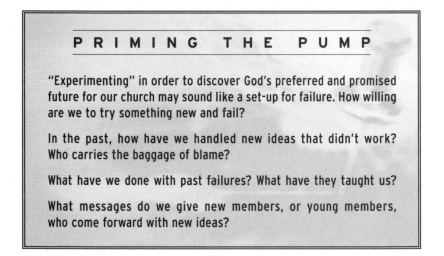

PRIMING THE PUMP

"Experimenting" in order to discover God's preferred and promised future for our church may sound like a set-up for failure. How willing are we to try something new and fail?

In the past, how have we handled new ideas that didn't work? Who carries the baggage of blame?

What have we done with past failures? What have they taught us?

What messages do we give new members, or young members, who come forward with new ideas?

PHASE 3: VISIONING FOR EMBODIMENT

IN MANY WAYS THIS CHAPTER describes the equivalent of what most models of congregational development and redevelopment offer as their whole proposal. This chapter also describes the huge difference between traditional organizational planning and doing these things within a spiritual journey in which a congregation discerns a missional vocation.

In this chapter I describe the process of creating a vision to be embodied through a strategic plan. On the whole the actions proposed here are very much like the actions of those other proposals, but these actions fit within a profoundly different model of change. By the time your congregation has come to this point on the journey of spiritual discernment, a number of realities are in place that make this process substantially different than if you were to do them right away. You probably can name these, but allow me to make a short list from my experience.

Congregations by this time have developed critical practices of spiritual discernment, including:

- *Dwelling in the Word.*

- *Listening one another into free speech.*

- *Praying together to discern God's preferred and promised future rather than asking God to bless anticipated outcomes.*

- *Recognizing the anxieties, fears, and memories that prevent trusting God's faithfulness.*

At this stage congregations have also developed leaders who:

- *Lead out of spiritual discernment.*

- *Lead out of personal daily spiritual practices beginning with Dwelling in the Word.*

- *Listen, interpret, and communicate within the biblical narrative.*

- *Have listened to the congregational culture.*

- *Have listened to the culture of those who the congregation believes God is calling them to serve.*

- *Narrate the numbers of the congregation and persons to be served in mission.*

- *Create an environment that affirms risk.*

- *Actively reflect upon their experiments.*

- *Are able to distinguish adaptive change from technical change.*

- *Conduct Missional Engagement Teams.*

- *Embrace the challenge of a New Missional Era.*

Hopefully your list could go on, but it is enough to say that you are ready for innovation. Now, when leaders invite the full participation of the congregation to develop a statement of missional vocation, a vision for embodying that mission, and a planning process for acting toward that embodiment, a critical mass of members share this sense of missional vocation.

Missional vocation is irreplaceable. Without a critical mass of church members sharing a sense that God is calling them to a specific part of God's mission, the creation of mission statements, visions for mission, and strategic plans will not move a congregation from maintenance of Christendom to a New Missional Era. The focus is not on getting some right words on paper but on capturing the imaginations and practices of this critical mass of members.

By critical mass we mean something very specific. We have found that 15-20 percent of active members is enough. By active members, we mean people in your average worship attendance. If your average worship attendance is 100, your active membership is 100. Whether

they are on your rolls as members or not means far less than whether they attend regularly. So the critical mass in this instance is 15-20 people. This follows the 80/20 principle; that is, 80 percent of the work in a local church is done by 20 percent of the membership. (Actually, we find it an even smaller percentage, closer to 10 percent in many congregations.)

The most difficult group to influence is those members who have for years faithfully conducted the work of the local church to maintain Christendom. They have given up major parts of their lives carrying on the practices of Christendom and are not likely to change. At best, we pray that their imaginations and hearts will find the missional vocation so compelling that they celebrate when others pick it up. Some of these truly faithful members will be able to join in the work of the New Missional Era.

TRUSTEES OF THE VISION

To this point we have spoken of many different leadership groups, groups we intentionally develop into significant relational groups. The Steering Team, Listening Leader Team, the governance board, and Missional Engagement Teams all are significant relational groups that are joining in a shared sense of missional vocation. I have also learned from decades of work in local churches and through a growing body of scholarship that a group I call "trustees of the vision" plays a critical role.

Trustees of the vision are not an elected group, unless one takes seriously their election by the Holy Spirit. These persons may or may not have held elective office in the local church. They may or may not be on the staff. They may or may not be known by the majority of the congregation. What they have in common is a clear sense of why their congregation exists, of what gives it a distinct identity and purpose. They have a sense of a vision of this identity and purpose for the future, and they are its trustees. They hold it in trust.

I vividly remember meeting Polly, a woman in her nineties, now blind. I visited her in her home, built by her husband and herself in the 1930s from stones on their land in the mountains of western Maryland. The young pastor had suggested I visit with her, even though it meant a major addition to my stay. As I sat with Polly, she began to describe why her church had survived many years in those mountains and why now it had a very different future. She recognized that the new neighbors, mostly people retiring to the mountains from the Washington, D.C./Baltimore metropolitan area, were a critical part of the future for her congregation. She knew that the newcomers made bad neighbors and that the members of the congregation thought so, too. She knew that this would be hard work for both groups but that it was God's will for them. She wisely described the obstacles, including particular families who had "run" the congregation. She included her own as a family that would need to give up much of what they valued to walk into God's preferred and promised future. She had this vision; it was remarkably clear. I had met others similar to her but no one quite like her. Since then I have learned to listen for them because in most congregations God provides them.

When it came time for the congregation to start this phase of PMC, Polly and a handful of other trustees of the vision were able to capture the imagination of the congregation. For Polly was not only a trustee of the vision; she was also a major influence broker in the congregation. You know the sort of persons I mean: before they speak, a lot of people have no opinion on a question, but after they speak, everyone has an opinion. When Polly articulated her sense of the purpose and identity of the congregation and how God was calling it to this new identity and purpose, members' hearts and imaginations were moved. She almost single-handedly created a sense of a compelling missional vocation.

The experience of Polly is not the norm, but it is not unusual. A handful of persons who hold the trust of the vision of a congregation can have tremendous influence for good or for ill.

I have seen trustees of a vision lead in a different direction, too. In one instance, in a southern California congregation that had been a mission start in the post-World War II boom, the descendants of the original mission developer were both trustees of the vision and influence brokers in the congregation. Worship attendance was down to them and a few others. The immediate community had changed vastly and several times. The value of the property upon which the worship space was built was very high, and members were tempted to sell it. While too long a story to tell well here, these trustees of the vision rejected a missional vision. This can happen, even at this late stage of the PMC process; however, it does not happen very often. Usually the rebellion against a sense of missional vocation will show itself earlier than at the beginning of the third phase.

CASTERS OF A VISION FOR EMBODIMENT

Other kinds of leaders play a significant role in this phase, as well. During this time, the casters of a vision for embodiment become very important. They themselves may not have a vision for the future of

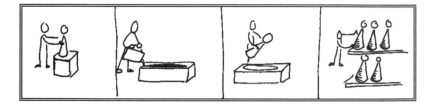

the congregation, but they have the gift to take that vision and begin to give it shape. You might think of them as casters of an already established piece of sculpture, or at least an already designed piece of sculpture.

My wife and I had the opportunity to visit Santa Fe when my wife was working in Zuni, New Mexico, with Indian Health Services. I was completing another book, *Welcoming the Stranger,* and had been deeply moved by a particular sculpture by Judith Klausner, a sculptor who lived six months a year in Santa Fe and six months in New York. She worked themes from the Hebrew scriptures, especially the patriarchal narratives and the life of David. My wife and I fell in love with a series around the life and Abraham and Sarah and through the gallery that handled her work we got to know her. We saw how she developed the original design as a purely imaginative concept, and then she made drawings that led to a wax sculpture that was used to establish a cast for the eventual bronze piece. This wax sculpture created the reverse cast in sand that would become the cast for the bronze. While her vision started within the biblical narrative and developed through temporary drawings, her ability to create a cast for her vision was a necessary, though temporary, step.

The spiritual journey of forming a missional vocation involves this same kind of process. What begins in Phase 1 within the biblical narrative, the narrative of the community and congregation, and the narrated numbers of the local church demographics and psychographics, moves through multiple experiments in Phase 2. In Phase 3 you will need casters of the Vision for Embodiment who offer a particular rendering of the missional vocation in a couple of paragraphs that will be tested within the life of the congregation and community. These leaders have a lively and realistic sense of the world and push specific questions whose answers give a specific sense of what that future missional vocation might look like. They, along with leaders who know how to integrate the political and social realities, join with those whose gifts are mostly of prayer and spiritual insight to create the five documents that move vision to embodied action. What begins in the imagination ends in spiritually strong but politically real action.

FIVE DOCUMENTS

In my earlier years of consulting with congregations, I did not respect the importance of regular written documents. So, for example, I did not value the importance of minutes for meetings and the importance of the role of secretary. Really significant leadership moments were lost because of this failure on my part.

As time went on, I began to appreciate more and more how well-documented meetings and decisions assisted forward movement like few other things could. As I noted when recounting the role of the senior pastor in a very large church that had gone through massive change over and over again, he consistently functioned as a secretary to what we call Missional Engagement Teams. As he said, "I reminded them what they had said and decided the last time we met. I defined and clarified what they were doing next and to what ends and purposes they were acting." He also interpreted those decisions, ends, and purposes within the biblical narrative of God's mission and helped them name their own missional vocation.

I have learned, similarly, that if you do not have written documents, it is very hard to maintain focus and accountability to a missional vocation. So, in Phase 3 we produce five documents:

1. Statement of Missional Vocation
2. Vision for Embodiment of Missional Vocation
3. Strategic Plan
4. SMART Plans of Action
5. Staff Covenant

1. STATEMENT OF MISSIONAL VOCATION

By now the concept of a missional vocation should be clear, but our experience shows this is an extremely difficult concept to understand and an even more difficult one to realize. The critical mass of

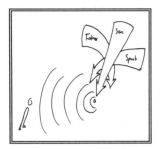

people needs to open themselves up to the possibility that God has a preferred future for their local church. A sense of false humility might prevent this from happening: namely, a significant number of people say, "We are not important enough for God to care about our particular local church in more than a general way." Or, they may say, "Yes, of course, God has a preferred future for our local church, but who are we to say what it is? God is hidden and does not reveal such things to us, certainly not specifically." Or, quite common, "We know what the general mission of the church is, and we are to do all of that in this location." This latter opinion reveals how deeply Christendom holds our imaginations and keeps us from seeing where we are in the history of the relationship between the local church and its culture and environment.

Most of the time, this language of mission elicits grand dreams rather than concrete, specific missional vocation. Try to avoid this trap. I know of several urban churches who have taken on such grand dreams. Some, following the pattern of national church bodies use the BHAG: Big Hairy Audacious Goals. This trap is especially dangerous. First, the BHAG model usually says things no one can possibly be against. Rejecting it would be like rejecting motherhood, apple pie, hot dogs, or Jesus. No Christian would want to be caught speaking against it. Second, the BHAG model can provide a certain energy for a period of time. It especially appeals to the sprinters who want to see real change, real fast. Third, it makes those in charge of the change feel good; they feel like they are doing something important, something that will make a difference. Fourth, it makes immediate political progress. When you are starting out, it is very important to get mighty momentum with you; the BHAG can give the impression you have that momentum since lots of people get excited about the BHAG.

These are not irrelevant factors in trying to establish momentum at the beginning of Visioning for Embodiment. Momentum is critical. Be that as it may, on the congregational level I have found it far, far better to get a critical mass focused on specific, concrete missional vocation that they can well imagine doing, though they will need to stretch and make adaptive change to accomplish it.

Allow me to tell the story of two urban Christendom congregations. One congregation once had 5,000 in worship attendance. This congregation served a missional vocation related to immigrants from northern Europe who already were members of their denomination. Through four generations, this local church provided state-of-the-art Christendom ministry, hiring the finest staff in classical music, childhood education, and many clergy specialists to carry out a level of professional services equal to the quality the middle- to upper-middle-class members enjoyed in other parts of their life.

However, as people moved to more distant suburbs, as younger generations valued less and less the "professional" approach and sought out churches where they were allowed to become more engaged in the ministry, or as folks simply dropped out of church, the congregation lost worship attendance. The stress upon staff became greater and greater, since they were still expected to provide professional services, to do the ministry for the congregation, "to perform the ministry" as one staff member summarized.

As members left, less income created the need to cut staff; the need to cut staff put more stress on existing staff. The natural tensions that exist in any group of people were intensified. Senior pastors began to "check out"; strong leaders left because of the constant conflict. The congregation brought in state-of-the-art conflict management consultants who lowered the anxiety in the system and restored a sense of tranquility, but the continuing spiral of doing more with less continued. New conflict arose.

The congregation hired consultants to work with the governance board to create a mission statement and a strategic plan. After a few retreats and a congregational meeting, attended by about 10 percent of active members, they announced their new mission statement and strategic plan. They completed a BHAG, put together a professional marketing and development plan, including a very aggressive capital fund drive, and rearranged staff to work on urban development projects with other local churches, forming a coalition with those churches.

After a year they evaluated how well the plan was going and found that only a couple of staff had accomplished their objectives and that worship attendance and active involvement in ministry had continued to drop. So, they simply increased pressure on staff, putting upon them clear objectives and deadlines. After six years of this process with growing failure and conflict, many staff able to get work elsewhere left. Many of those who remained admitted in interviews conducted by Church Innovations that they had in their hearts retired.

Starting with the staff and a couple members of the governance board, a new missional vision began to take shape. The pressure to produce quick fixes was tremendous as a new senior pastor arrived and old patterns of hiring staff to do the ministry remained in the imagination of many lay leaders. Against the pressure, staff and those few members of the governance board stuck with the first two phases of the PMC spiritual journey.

This time, when they were ready to write a missional vocation statement, they had developed a critical mass of members who believed God was calling them to a particular missional vocation. They were able to describe in very concrete terms what that missional vocation was because they had engaged in Missional Engagement Teams, one of which had discovered an important match of the gifts of the Spirit; the passions of a large number of members; and the strengths, hurts, and hopes of a group of unchurched persons in their service area.

Their strengths of music and the arts, which had suffered under constant attack as irrelevant to the poor and contemporary urbanite, found a critical role in this missional vocation. To be sure, that role was very different from the role it had played when servicing the original immigrant population, but as the music director noted, "We have taken a piece of our past, a gift God has given us, and made it a part of God's preferred future."

A critical mass of this local church now sees themselves as the primary ministers, and they look to staff as those who coach and provide the infrastructure for multiplying their ministry. Staff spends more time coaching and teaching than "doing the ministry for the people," and this has meant some hard adjustments for some. Together they find ways of innovating missional church along the lines of their spiritually discerned missional vocation. Evaluation and assessment still have their place, but staff and congregation create the tools and process together, and the long patterns that led to conflict and burnout are dying.

Another urban congregation had served a group of rural immigrants who had moved to the big city during the Great Depression.
They had made a little home away from home for persons of their
religious and cultural tradition in a place where they could find work.
By the 1990s this congregation was down to roughly 12 regular worshipers. They knew who they were and carried on a vital ministry for
themselves but were not at peace with the likelihood that their congregation would die in the next few years.

They started a process of spiritual discernment, asking themselves
and God what their missional vocation was. They experimented with
some of the ideas they found promising. After a few experiments, they
came to the common discernment that God had made them experts
at being strangers in a strange land and community. They looked
around them and saw thousands upon thousands of very recent immigrants to their city and tried some experiments at forming Christian
community with them.

To make a long and fascinating story very short, my colleague John
Mueller Nowell and I had the pleasure of worshiping with this congregation in their new $4.2 million worship and community center
with more than 400 persons in attendance from 16 cultures, speaking
11 different languages. A number of the original 12 members remain
active, while leadership is shared with new generations and new cultures that only the Holy Spirit could have formed into missional
community. While this community faces tremendous challenges as it
seeks to govern itself with such different cultural expectations and
languages, our interviews in this congregation indicate a deep and
wide conviction of their shared missional vocation.

In each case, they did what you will do. They wrote in a sentence
or two a sense of what God is calling them to do with specific persons
within their service area. These paragraphs are not BHAGs, but grew
out of some early trials to discern God's preferred future among them.
They have a concrete sense of a useable past in their future. They are

able to say "no" to good things they might otherwise do because, on the basis of these two paragraphs, they know their own specific vocation. They can healthily avoid the temptation to do everything, to become the spiritual filling station for a Christendom community.

2. VISION FOR EMBODIMENT OF MISSIONAL VOCATION

More and more I am convinced that leadership is primarily about time, not position; it is a temporal and relational reality more than it is a positional reality. If a person has the trust of a community and a sense of vision, that person can lead from many different positions within the organization. And, if a person does not have the trust of a community and/or little or no sense of vision, it is very difficult for that person to lead regardless of position within the organization.

When a local church has established a Steering Team and Listening Leader Team in conjunction with the governance board, and balanced them with the sprinters through the Missional Engagement process, and further engaged a critical mass of active members in forming a shared missional vocation, it is important for leaders to state in clear and simple terms what this missional vocation might look like, embodied, in three to five years. This document speaks of the local church as it forms missional Christian community three to five years in the future. It envisions actual people practicing missional community with those to whom they believe Jesus is sending them in mutual mission.

This document describes three to five primal practices (big rocks) as they will be embodied at the end of three to five years. What will worship look like as you embody your missional voca-

tion? What will a couple of the other primal practices of forming missional community look like? How will you make disciples and send apostles? What will your engagement with civil society look like? Here the work of the first two phases—the study of the culture of the service area and the culture of the local church, the discovery of partners who can build bridges, the sense of gifts and passions—takes on flesh and blood in imagined missional practices and patterns.

3 . STRATEGIC PLAN

This document takes the Vision for Embodiment and imagines the step-by-step process of getting from where you are to that first major stage of embodying your missional vocation three to five years down the road. If you are to shape worship as a public witness and not just the support of a closed system, the family, how might you incrementally develop your capacities to do so? What needs to be done in these three to five years to get there? In the first year? In the first six months? In the next six weeks?

Strategic plans are working documents for maintaining focus and  managing attention. The further out you go in time with a strategic plan, the less accurate it can be, but it can nonetheless provide a place you intend to go and a way of focusing your attention upon it. You may need to update your strategic plan from time to time, but it is important to use to it consistently and not be constantly rewriting it.

A well-written strategic plan can focus the attention of every part of the local church's organization. The governance board should attend to it in planning, executing, and evaluating every meeting. Quarterly evaluations and assessments seem to work well in the first couple years that a strategic plan is used. At least one major retreat for governing board and staff should focus on evaluation and assessment of work accomplished through the strategic plan. As a tool for managing attention, I have found strategic plans invaluable.

4 .   S M A R T   P L A N S   O F   A C T I O N

This is a term used by many organizations, but in PMC it has definitions that differ from most applications of this concept, and they come with practices. In PMC, SMART Plans of Action are documents created for planning what will be done between the present group meeting and the next one. The primary purpose of SMART Plans of Action is to put the focus upon getting things done between meetings rather than the very, very bad habit in church circles of thinking that the important work is done only in the meet-  ings. The result of this bad habit is meetings that pile up good things we should be doing, passing motions to do them, and then returning to the next meeting to discover that little or nothing has happened in between. Of course, since the things we said we would do are good, we reaffirm them with several other good ideas, and eventually we stop expecting them to get done and let them fall into the dustbin of good intentions.

Using SMART Plans of Action can shorten your list and get more of the good things done. What follows is a short explanation of the SMART Plan.

S = Specific concrete objective

If we don't state what we are trying to get done between now and the next meeting, we are not likely to get it (or anything else) done. At best, nothing happens; at worst, people use time and resources working at something that does not further the missional vocation or our desire to embody it. Being able to state in a short sentence the specific concrete objective can avoid both of these pitfalls.

The objective should be so specific and concrete that you will know whether it has been done. For example: "Create a team of five people to form a Missional Engagement Team to explore alternative worship." "Contact the new county commissioner about the amount of, availability of, and process of applying for support for food shelves." "Invite one choir member with the gift of prayer to shape the prayer life of the choir."

M = Missional

The specific, concrete objectives need to fit within the missional vocation and the Vision for Embodiment. Before a SMART Plan of Action can be adopted, it must be clear where it fits within the missional vocation and the strategic plan. Nothing wastes more energy, time, and hope in local churches than doing too many things that don't synergize with missional vocation. This is tough work and can create significant tension in a meeting. New members might experience this process as a way of excluding their new ideas and, alas, if poorly used, it can be just that. Those who have for years maintained Christendom will experience this as one more place where the new "ruling coalition" is controlling everything in the congregation. Others will say, "This gives little room for the Holy Spirit to move us in different directions." Each of these challenges becomes a delightful opportunity to test the Spirit and the sense of missional vocation. Handled well, each of these challenges generates energy for mission.

A = Authorization and accountability

Once again, I have found that committees and boards in congregations often pass motions without providing for authorization to get something done. They do not provide the focus, energy, resources, or political authority to get the job done. They pass a motion saying they want this good thing to happen. They might even appoint a committee to do it. This makes me especially nervous because when a whole committee in a church is authorized to do something, it seldom happens. If two people are authorized to do something, it happens as much as half the time. If, however, one person is authorized to see that something happens, it often happens.

Now, I want to be clear here. When I say a person is "authorized to see that something happens," I do not mean that the person has to do it all. Indeed, if a group of people authorizes someone to see that something happens, in principle that group frees that person to get in their faces and say, "I need your help to do this part of the action." The group also authorizes that person to speak on behalf of the committee. Such authorization has its dangers. People who are not respectful of boundaries and limits might use such authorization in ways harmful to Christian community.

Such possible abuse and, more importantly, the need to appreciate and celebrate the successful completion of a specific concrete missional objective demonstrate the importance of accountability, the second "A" in SMART Plan of Action. When authorizing someone to see that something happens, it is important also to state clearly to whom the authorized person is accountable. Is it the chair of the committee doing the authorization? Is it a member of staff? The answer may vary, but in each case it should serve to synergize staff and members in missional community.

R = Resources

Resources are obvious. Make sure to list them, though. How much money will it take to do this specific concrete missional objective? Who will need to give time to make this work? How will the plan draw upon existing resources, and what kind of resources will need to be developed?

Time and hope are the extremely valued resources in any congregation. We can spend them unwisely doing things that, while good, do not focus and synergize missional community. The amount of time and hope relates, also, to the individuals and groups being asked to invest them. Given people's self-understanding of their gifts and passions, they might well be willing to give much more time and energy to one specific concrete missional objective than to another. We often ignore this matching of passions and gifts to the broader missional vocation.

T = Timeline

Before adopting any specific concrete missional objective, work out a timeline for its accomplishment with the last point on the timeline being the next meeting of the group to whom the authorized person is accountable. The sooner that next meeting is, the more likely something is to be accomplished. Of course, some specific concrete missional objectives may need to be broken down into distinct steps. Then the SMART Plan of Action might indicate a future date for other steps, but it must include a timeline between the present meeting and the next group meeting. If you do not use the timeline function in this manner, SMART Plans of Action start to become mini strategic plans, and this often defeats their purpose.

5. STAFF COVENANT

More than 20 years ago, I started working with staffs of large churches, helping them do in-service training, job descriptions, spiritual retreats, and work organization. Early in those days, I was very influenced by the work of a friend and colleague, Anne Marie Neuchterlein, a pastor who holds a Ph.D. in family systems counseling. Borrowing from her insights, putting them together with the long-standing work of biblical scholars on covenanting, small professional group organizational models, and the patterns of missional church, we built the process that creates this document.

The document engages staff—full- or part-time, supportive or programmatic—in a set of two or three two-day retreats. In these retreats they dwell in the Word of God, especially scriptures teaching about covenants and how they work in the missional community.

Covenants are ways God holds us accountable and ways we hold each other accountable within a system of mercy, a system of accountability and forgiveness. Healthy missional staffs recognize that they need accountability. If they avoid accountability, they are harmed individually and as a group, the congregation is harmed, and the development of missional community is impeded.

Accountability is learned, both overtly and covertly, in our family of origin. Local church staff members need to reflect upon those patterns so they can faithfully, effectively, and efficiently hold one another accountable in a way that the mercy of God has the last word. Retreat participants spend time looking at family systems patterns and then seeing how they work out in staff systems.

Job descriptions are transformed into job authorizations. We compare what staff are supposed to be doing with what they are truly free and authorized to do and find ways of assessing and evaluating those authorizations in relation to the local church's missional vocation. Using tried-and-true methods of time logs and assessment of gifts and passions, staff members create a set of job authorizations and a plan for staff development.

This set of job authorizations, representing all staff, along with a staff development plan, is appended to a clear statement of the covenant the staff is willing to live by as its part of the missional vocation of the congregation. The covenant includes values and practices that will shape how the staff relates to one another and to the governance system of the congregation. On the basis of this staff covenant, local church leaders can discern places where the staff needs development, where new staff need to be recruited, and where members of the congregation can integrate their gifts and passions into the shared journey.

ART AND POLITICS

In the summer before my junior year in high school, I lived with a family on the south side of Chicago. During that summer, I encountered many cultural boundaries. One of them happened quite unexpectedly when my "brother" Roger and I visited the Art Institute of Chicago. For both of us, French art was an undiscovered culture. We entered a room filled with French impressionist and expressionist art. He and I soon became mesmerized by a piece by Monet. If we 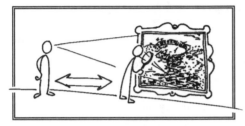 stood close to the painting, it appeared to be a bunch of strokes of bright paint on canvas; the bunch of strokes became a village and hillside when we backed away from the painting. We moved back and forth, experiencing again and again the moment when the brush strokes became a discernible set of images, the moment when the strokes became a whole for us. We would then move closer and see how each of the brush strokes contributed to the whole. This moving back and forth, from whole to detail, went on for at least 45 minutes. We were totally captivated.

Over the years, I have watched congregations go through this same process from whole to detail, from a sense of their missional vocation to particular parts of a vision for mission and a strategic plan to the even finer details of SMART Plans of Action. Some who do the work are convinced it is simply a linear process, almost expecting the discernment to be like painting by the numbers. Some think of it as a purely "irrational" and nonlinear process that takes place in the imagination of a few creative persons who deliver the vision to the rest. In neither case will a lively, compelling missional vocation become embodied. No, it is neither a paint-by-the-numbers process nor an irrational imaginative process. It requires both a sense of the whole picture and the step-by-step filling in of the particulars. Leaders in the process will need to step close and then back, over and over again as the whole and the pieces fall together. When it works, leaders require both people who need the step-by-step details and people who can catch the vision and pass it on.

Art and politics go together rather than being enemies. Spiritual discernment is both imaginative and practical. A variety of gifts and a lot of patience and impatience go together to embody the missional vocation. I have learned that a vision without a  plan of action is but a dream. A plan of action without a vision gets you nowhere but with a longer list of things to do. A vision with a plan of action, however, can change your world. Opening yourself up to the guidance of the Holy Spirit while keeping a clear eye for the individual pieces and how they relate makes it happen. God is in both the big picture and the details.

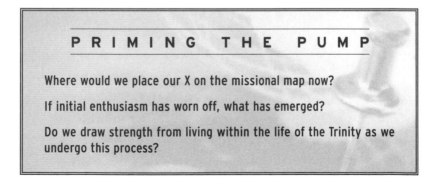

P R I M I N G   T H E   P U M P

Where would we place our X on the missional map now?

If initial enthusiasm has worn off, what has emerged?

Do we draw strength from living within the life of the Trinity as we undergo this process?

CHAPTER 6

PHASE 4: LEARNING AND GROWING

BY THE TIME A CONGREGATION has adopted its five documents (Statement of Missional Vocation, Vision for Embodiment, Strategic Plan, SMART Plans of Action, and Staff Covenant), the congregation has both a sense of focus and purpose and a clear awareness of many things it does not know. At this point in the spiritual journey, the congregation can make a better judgment as to what it:

- *does know;*
- *doesn't know;*
- *doesn't even know it doesn't know;*
- *needs to know to grow into what it has discerned is God's preferred and promised future.*

In short, it needs continuing education. It may need to learn more about the role of significant relational groups, worship as public witness, gift assessment, ministries in day-to-day life, anti-racism, spiritual direction, and so on.

Rather than simply making a list of things to learn, however, congregational leaders have formed a learning community with those they believe God has sent them to join in doing the mission of God.

CHANGE AS LISTS OF THINGS TO DO   CHANGE AS A JOURNEY OF DISCOVERY

From this insight of spiritual discernment, this congregation, with its cluster partners, creates an ongoing continuing education plan. They can learn with and from one another, and share costs through the learning community.

Within this learning community, a reflective model of learning is in place. Continuing education moves beyond an ad hoc decision based on what seems interesting, well-known, provided by a preferred

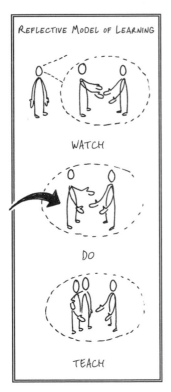

REFLECTIVE MODEL OF LEARNING

WATCH

DO

TEACH

vendor (church consultant, churchwide staff, judicatory staff, favorite professor or theological school, latest business trend, and so on), or required for certification. Continuing education belongs to the congregation's life as a learning community. It has a wide scope and depth but a clear purpose and focus. It grows out of a defined missional vocation and a clear path for walking together into God's preferred and promised future.

At this point in the PMC spiritual journey, continuing education includes a wide variety of leaders in the congregation, not just the "paid staff." One of the easiest ways I check on whether a congregation has become a missional learning community is by determining if these values are present: each Christian is a missionary in day-to-day life, and it is the responsibility of the congregation to provide continuing education for them. From this I can see the degree to which the congregation has come to understand that the church is church, whether gathered or sent, and missional all the time.

As a result, those who attend the Learning and Growing cluster events are highly motivated to learn and to put what they learn into action. As Dr. Pat Taylor Ellison taught me early on in our work together, "Adults learn what they want to learn, not what we want to teach them." Since the curriculum of the Learning and Growing cluster events is created from the sense of missional vocation and the congregation's plans to embody it, people show up for the events ready to learn and ready to make it work. This makes Phase 4 cluster events high-powered learning functions.

Even though congregations often choose to create a continuing education process that takes up common topics, they do so within a missional church framework. This framework includes certain components and methods of learning—practices and habits for acting, reflecting, and constructing local theology out of a conversation with those the congregation is serving in mission.

The focuses of the first three phases of the shared spiritual journey were (1) listening to discover our missional partners; (2) risking through experimenting with missional adaptive challenges; and (3) discerning a missional vocation and creating shared practical documents for embodying it in the near future. The underlying framework of spiritual discernment should continue to shape the Learning  and Growing Phase of PMC. Indeed, it might become more consciously present in the work of a handful of leaders in each congregation and those outside the congregation who work with those leaders.

Although continuing education topics vary from cluster to cluster, certain topics are common. What follows are some of those topics.

WORSHIP AS PUBLIC WITNESS AND COMMUNITY FORMATION

Often congregations want to act and reflect on worship as mission. They want their worship to be an effective public witness to the triune God. They want a sense of Christian hospitality to be the

woof and warp of their worship practices. They are also aware that, although there are common practices of hospitality and of public witness that are embodied in the broad patterns of historic Christian

worship, truly public worship engages the actual persons who gather for worship and those they believe Jesus is sending them to serve in God's mission. Above all, they know that worship is not simply an instrument or tool of the church, local or universal, that can be used to either maintain community or convert neighbors.

Indeed, within a missional church framework, instrumental notions of worship are replaced with missional ones. God is the chief actor in Christian worship, and God is calling, gathering, centering, and sending people in the movement and practices of Christian worship. Christian worship follows from the movement and sending of God, the very life of the Trinity. As a result, all Christian worship is forming community within the life of the Trinity.

Imagine a congregation that has dwindled to 20 worshipers from 1,400 on an average Sunday. It has moved from vibrant family and youth involvement to a congregation whose median age is 67. Imagine that it literally has its foundation sinking into sand and faces a minimum $150,000 bill to keep it from continuing to sink. Even the banks in the area, eager to stabilize their community, especially its real estate, refuse to lend the money to the congregation to stop the sinking.

Imagine that the congregation takes the chance of opening itself to the missional vocational question, "What is God calling us to do in mission?" They dwell in the Word over a number of months, struggle with their own sense of failure and despair, and face tough questions about their own sense of purpose.

Out of this listening and discovering of possible partners within their congregation, within their community, with other congregations, and most importantly, with God, they decide to try some experiments. They learn that the second highest concentration of children between ages 0-4 in their metropolitan area is within a 15-minute walking distance from their sinking buildings. Further, through listening to these children's parents, they discover the need for support in parenting, especially since most of the parents are single with very limited financial resources and support systems. Equally important, their own members have a heart for these children and their parents.

The first experiment they want to try is fairly typical: preschool day care. However, the Missional Engagement Team assigned to the task discovers that it will cost a minimum of $75,000 to bring their building up to codes set by their local government to house preschool day care. As noted earlier, they do not have the money to fix their foundation. They certainly don't have the money to do the necessary upgrades for a day care.

Their initial response is despair, but they are convinced that God is calling them to serve this group of children and their parents. So the team explores further. They discover another approach, far cheaper but more immediately responsive to the needs of the parents and children.

They start a babysitting service, a Parents' Night Out, on Saturday nights—free babysitting from 6 to 11 p.m., provided by a team of one elder and two young adults. They pay for training through a local agency that certifies young adults for babysitting. This allows the young adults to eventually charge more for their own babysitting jobs while providing for their supervised babysitting through the Parents' Night Out.

They recruit and train eight teams of three. This allows teams to work only one Saturday out of eight. The burden is relatively light.

They put up announcements in the local launderettes, grocery stores, and so forth. They return to the parents who had participated in the listening process to let them know they were heard. The numbers that turn out are strong but within their capacity to provide a healthy service.

At the end of the first year, the congregation sponsors a picnic for all the parents and children who have been a part of the Parents' Night Out. More than 180 show up for the picnic!

Church Innovations interviewed more than 90 parents who used the service and asked if they would mind if the children were taught Bible stories and Christian hymns. (The congregation had insisted that nothing explicitly Christian be a part of the Parents' Night Out.) All but one noted they would welcome their children being taught. Many assumed that since they were bringing their children to a church, it was already happening.

In light of this information and the strong positive feelings generated by the first year of Parents' Night Out, leaders decided to sponsor a worship service each Saturday night. The service starts at 5:30 p.m. and includes the children and babysitters. Within weeks a regular congregation was born complete with worship and a sense of shared purposes. During the year, parents using the Parents' Night Out started taking "their turns" on Saturday nights. Some sought adult learning through small groups. Within the first year, three sought to become Christian and dozens of children were added to the worship service. In short, a new worship service related to this new congregation was established. This is missional worship; it reflects the congregation's missional vocation formed in relationships with persons the congregation believed God was calling them to serve in mission.

On the basis of the experiment and the growing engagement with the community, at least two other things took place. The local bank saw a community worth investing in. They loaned the congregation the money to secure the foundation. Several of the older members of the congregation gained a sense of a future for their congregation, and they left in their wills more than enough to pay off the new debt and significant support for the new emerging congregation. This is just one of many examples of congregations that have developed missional worship, worship that is a public witness to God's mission and the congregation's missional vocation.

THE BIBLE AND CHRISTIAN FORMATION

Hopefully by this fourth phase of the PMC spiritual journey the role and place of the Bible in forming Christian community within the life of the Trinity has become common practice. The way the Bible is used probably reveals as clearly as anything how the congregation truly believes God is related to the world.

If the Bible is only used for study (an admirable purpose), the congregation believes that the primary way God relates to the world is through study. Used in this way, the Bible usually remains the prisoner of the assumptions of modernity, the notion that true knowledge about God must fit into the category of facts and be  subject to being "studied"; that is, the Bible is an object at hand and within the grasp and control of the student.

Strangely, this approach has captured the imagination of most moderns, conservative and liberal. These two groups may come to very different conclusions on the basis of their turning the Bible into an object of study, but they agree on the primary modern understanding of the use of the Bible.

To be sure, most conservatives believe the facts they uncover are, as they are apt to say, "literally true." Most liberals reject those conclusions and suggest that the Bible is not very useful for such facts but can be a powerful source for the facts of the faith of those who wrote the Bible. Liberals are more likely to focus on experience, especially their own, against such literalism. In the analysis that stands behind a missional church vision, however, both of these movements, conservative and liberal, represent the colonization of Christian community and faith by modern European/American culture.

In practical terms, our studies at Church Innovations lead us to believe that this modernist approach turns the Bible into a toolbox. When conflict arises in a local church, the toolbox approach often turns the Bible into ammunition. Both sides of a question—and too often local churches believe there are only two sides to a question—run to the Bible as their ammunition. They load their guns with Bible bullets and arrive for the conversation ready to fire. Needless to say, using Bible bullets seldom leads to life-giving conversation. Bullets are, after all, designed to kill. So, whether liberal or conservative, using the Bible this way kills.

Even if a modernist is offended by the Bible bullet practice, he or she is likely to be unable to propose an alternative. Instead, such a person is likely to pour pious syrup on the conversation with pronouncements, often in a pleading tone. "Doesn't the Bible say God is love? Why don't we stop fighting and just love one another?" Such pronouncements kill life-giving conversation as fast as Bible bullets. After all, what reply can you make to such a question without harming the conversation further?

By this phase, the practices growing out of Dwelling in the Word have formed better ways of using the Bible, ways that grow out of deeper Christian traditions. Listening one another into free speech;

learning to dwell within culture, society, tradition, and the experience of the faithful (both communal and personal); and asking missional questions have transformed the basic prac- tices of forming Christian discipleship and community. A critical mass of leaders has learned to ask, "What is God doing here? How is God calling, gathering, centering, and sending us into God's mission?" They have learned how to dwell in God's Word,  to have the biblical narrative, by the power of the Holy Spirit, narrate their lives.

Christian worship that has the woof and warp of this narrative resists being turned into a tool or instrument. The Bible similarly resists being turned into a tool or instrument at hand to do something else. Of course, without a keen sense of this biblical narrative and the practice of Dwelling in the Word, local churches become easy prey for instrumentalism.

MAKING CHRISTIANS AND DOING LOCAL THEOLOGY

At some point in the PMC journey, most congregations discover that they need to learn and grow in their ability to form Christian community. They especially understand that forming Christian com- munity with and on behalf of those who have never, or only tangentially, listened to the biblical narrative profoundly shapes and strengthens their already existing community. Rather than building up the existing community against a terrible, faithless, ugly, and sinful world, congregations realize that forming Christian community within the life of the Trinity is done by joining God's mission in the world. Indeed, when a congregation learns to see, experience, and narrate a faithful, beautiful, and sacred world with those who have not come to this spiritual insight, I experience the greatest thrill of my work.

The business of forming Christian community is always about the catechumenate, about initiating persons into the reign of God through evangelism and a deliberate spiritual journey that takes them from being seekers (consumers of religion as commodity) to being disciples of Jesus. Forming Christian community without this basic activity leaves the congregation without the profound engagement of real people who seek to truly understand God.

Some congregations may do it better than others, but all missional congregations shape their life out of this catechetical movement. The

catechetical movement might be understood simply as the process of offering Christian answers to the frequently asked questions (FAQs) of real people seeking to understand God. Without the capacity of listening another into free speech, most congregations won't even hear the frequently asked questions. Without the capacity to dwell in the Word of God, congregations cannot offer Christian answers to those FAQs.

Seeking to truly understand God is done through spiritual discernment and critical reflection. Doing spiritual discernment and critical reflection within this missional community is doing theology, local theology. As a systematic theologian, I have sought to return theology in a practical and critical form to the life of local churches. In doing so, the capacities and practices of doing theology inherent in Christian community have become clearer and clearer to me. I have experienced the power of the Holy Spirit to maintain the church in truth and love while allowing the church to risk and fail. The Learning and Growing Phase, while focused on particular tasks, helps congregations do more and more practical, critical, innovative local theology.

RISK TAKING AS CONTRAST COMMUNITY

Another delightful pattern I have seen happen in congregations by this time in the PMC journey follows from being able to view the immediate environment from within the biblical narrative. Congregational leaders begin to see God's work in the world more readily, and they feel permission, indeed authorization, to risk participating in God's mission in the world.

This freedom grows out of their deep sense of being joined to the life of the Trinity through their sharing in the life, death, resurrection, and ascension of Jesus. They have a deepened sense of identity in Christ; they have a sense of authorization that frees them to a proper confident witness. They have risked failure, experienced it, and learned from it. They are open to risks that are in deep contrast to the basic patterns and values

of the culture in which they live. Rather than only fearing failure, or getting caught up in the sin and destruction of the culture in which they live, they also fear God; indeed, they fear God more than they fear failure and the power of sin, death, and the consumer society within which they live.

I have experienced congregations at this point being able to see various powers and principalities that they have feared more than God. Instead of being driven by guilt and condemnation, they are freed to witness to their own captivity to these powers and principalities. They want to learn more about these powers, but even more they want to grow into a contrast community that struggles against them.

The experience of our PMC journey in southern Africa reveals these dynamics of struggle against power and principalities and of taking the risk to become a contrast community. Without ignoring these same dynamics in my own culture, I have seen them more clearly and in greater relief in southern Africa. I have experienced congregations gathering for the first time who, although worshiping together, were divided by culture, class, race, and gender, a division intensified by the diversity of styles of music and ritual. Representatives of those local congregations huddled around tables looking around the room and at me as the presenter but not at one another. Indeed, I learned a hundred new ways of communicating with body language, facial movements, and speech: We do not like being with these other people. We are anxious and perhaps frightened. We thought the idea of working together across class, culture, and denominational lines was good, but now that we are here, it feels unsafe. We will not be rude to this white North American but we will not return a second time.

Those same persons were put into dyads around the Word of God and given the clear rules for practicing Dwelling in the Word and listening one another into free speech. Then, as a block of ice begins to melt, they began to dwell with one another. If only for a few moments, they later reported, they sat and listened to someone whom they had never listened to about such important things. They leaned into their "other," neither erasing the difference by pretending they were identical, nor running from the difference as if it were a threat. From these tepid, ice-melting moments of Dwelling in the Word and listening one another into free speech to mutual recognition of the partners God was providing them, the body language changed, slowly, but it changed indeed.

Later, in the anxiety and fear of risking failure in Phase 2, the constant self-consciousness began to recede and the mutual task of being missional church took up more time and energy. Congregations that were formed against one another and maintained against one another as a part of Apartheid policy and practice engaged in mutual risk through adaptive missional projects.

Within this spiritual journey, without ever running from or denying the powers and principalities, local church leaders were freed to name the powers and principalities through conversations about what God was calling them to do in mission. The focus was on God's Word, and God's mission created the safe space to confront the powers and principalities in their own lives. The tasks of listening to their communities and hearing and feeling the hurts and hopes of those people to whom they discerned God was sending them allowed the movement of God to be experienced more than the movement of those powers and principalities.

Almost all of the hundreds of congregations with whom we have journeyed in southern Africa have chosen to risk crossing those boundaries of class and culture in their Missional Engagement Teams and long-range plans. In almost every instance they enter the Learning and Growing Phase with a desire to understand more deeply the powers and principalities and to work together with those from whom they have been divided by those powers and principalities. Together they trust God's power revealed in the Crucified, Resurrected, and Ascended One—the power of the Holy Spirit. They consciously work on anti-racism training. They seek ways of understanding together the power of class to destroy life. They move beyond the easy answers of politicians, without demeaning the struggle of politics, because they know that this is primarily a journey of the Spirit.

DEPENDENCE ON THE SPIRIT

One of the most powerful theological insights for me in these 25 years has been that this is primarily a journey of the Holy Spirit. As a modern theologian I actually had a hard time integrating the Holy Spirit into my working theology. Please don't misunderstand me. I did not deny the doctrine of the Trinity. I did not ignore the power of the Holy Spirit in people's lives and in the local churches in which they gathered. I surely believed that it was by the power of the Holy Spirit that all of this happened.

However, it is one thing to affirm a doctrine and assert practical implications of that doctrine. It is quite another thing to experience and reflect upon the character of God as Triune; how God is present in every moment and place by the power of the Holy Spirit. How it is the Spirit that empowers the dance of Father, Son, and Holy Spirit. How God's being as communion profoundly resists my constant habit of conceiving of God as unitarian, despite my orthodox commitments.

How different it is to believe that the power of the Spirit maintains the church in truth and love, not infallibly but without fail or indefectibly; that is, no failure or defect of the church will prevent the Holy Spirit from maintaining the church in truth and love. How different it is to believe that the future of the people of God is within the people of God. How different it is for a theologian and consultant learning to do theology in, with, under, for, and against local churches.

This dependence on the Holy Spirit permeates every moment of PMC, whether it is the way we engage congregations or the way we  relate them to one another or the way we conceive of and work with the other systems of the church that support the PMC journey. Each congregation either recognizes this dependence or loses its way on the journey.

Time and time again, the temptation to turn this process into win/lose politics illustrates the significance of dependence upon the Holy Spirit in missional church. I have seen thoughtful and faithful church leaders become cynical, or worse, become practical atheists because they are unable to believe that the future of the people of God is among the people of God. They are unable to believe that dependence upon the Holy Spirit is practical.

Instead, when asked to open the process of conversation and struggle over power that is part of all human community, to open themselves up to the question of God's preferred and promised future, they say often bluntly, "That only changes the question to a pious one. It does not change the reality of the power struggle. Now, we will not fight about whose view on what we should be doing wins or loses; instead, we will fight about whose view on what God's preferred and promised future is wins or loses."

Of course, if it is all about win/lose politics, and if power cannot be ordered to a shared mission but rather is its own end, those leaders are right. However, they are also revealing either their cynicism or their belief that power is the ultimate truth. Such persons are practical atheists and also, more often than not, practical nihilists. They believe there is no reality we can know truly. There is no meaning greater than the will to power. I have met such persons in leadership at every level of the church and in almost every denomination and culture. These experiences have all the more convinced me of the power of the Holy Spirit and our dependence on that power to be missional church.

WITNESSING THE REIGN OF GOD

The obvious sometimes needs stating. Throughout the entire PMC spiritual journey, participants are invited, cajoled, pressed, encouraged, and even begged to wake up and witness the reign of God. I choose the verb wake because it describes my own sense of what happens to participants through the process, and it reminds me of Jesus inviting, cajoling, pressing, encouraging, indeed begging his disciples to 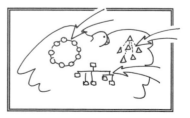 stay awake, especially in the Garden of the Mount of Olives. Through the years, I have found that a major part of the colonization by

Western modernity has been this falling asleep, this drowsiness to the life of the Trinity. In our legitimate desire to avoid violence due to religious fervor, we have deliberately tranquilized ourselves from witnessing the reign of God. In our desire for peace and justice (Who could be against them?), we have deadened our desire for beauty, for fearing and trusting in God above all things. Peace and justice, graces of the reign of God, become our gods.

Think of the reign of God being the space, time, authority, and movement of the Trinity. I realize this is an oversimplification, but for a bit let's work with this. We Christians believe we live within the life of the Trinity. We believe that God, Father, Son, and Holy Spirit create all things, seen and unseen. Yet, we have tranquilized ourselves to keep peace, to avoid religious violence, rather than making peace, trusting in the Holy Spirit's powers. We seldom see God's movement, authority, time, and space in the world.

Nowhere is this more obvious than in our modern aesthetic sensibilities. Imagine just a portion of the aesthetic price we pay for our drowsiness, our tranquilizing ourselves: most of our time and space become empty of beauty, and instead time and space get turned into commodities to control for production of things that add value to the economy. We believe adding value to the economy creates, in and of itself, peace and justice. We place efficiency over beauty in public and private space, especially at work, and even at home.

More astounding still, we even place efficiency over beauty when we worship the creator of all beauty. We are so drowsy, so tranquilized, we expect worship to be one more time and place where we are entertained, educated, given something useful in our self-improvement projects so we might be more productive in adding value to the economy. We hear the ancient promises that the Lord's Supper is a foretaste of the feast to come, a dwelling in eternity, but we skip celebrating the Lord's Supper for efficiency's sake. We even become so tranquilized to God's abundance of grace that we limit celebrating Holy Communion to four times a year or once a month, as if it could possibly become less meaningful to us by doing it every Sunday, as if dwelling in God's space and time could possibly happen too often.

We are, by many social science accounts, a people starving to death for time. Even those among us who are retired believe they do not have enough hours in the day. We even subsume time into a commodity we spend and are con-

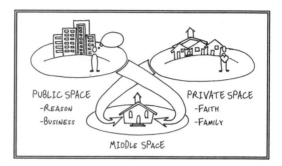

PUBLIC SPACE
  —REASON
  —BUSINESS

PRIVATE SPACE
  —FAITH
  —FAMILY

MIDDLE SPACE

stantly trying to buy more time to spend. Our drowsiness keeps us from witnessing the reign of God as a gift of eternal life, all the space and time we could possibly need, want, or desire.

Many among us who have not completely lost our sense of beauty try to buy it and make it our private possession. Art becomes something to collect, to own, to possess, and occasionally something to show off. We have so privatized our sense of beauty that we believe it belongs to a select few artists, those few people who have imaginations. We have lost our sense as poets, created co-creators of beauty. We can buy beauty from them if we have the money.

We even believe that beauty is in the eye of the beholder, completely making beauty a private possession. We may have put ourselves in such a deep sleep that we literally cannot see, feel, taste, and delight in the beauty of the creation. We have turned desire and delight in the beauty of the creation into a private reality and fail to witness the reign of God.

I use this example to illustrate our modern obsessions of allowing politics and economics to become a means of salvation, and making God's gifts of peace and justice grounds for idolatry and blasphemy.

So much more could and should be said. However, it is enough to illustrate why the spiritual journey of PMC begs participants to wake up, attend to the life of the Trinity, stay with Jesus a few minutes a week, and witness the reign of God.

WITNESS AND EVANGELISM

Many persons with whom I have worked assume within this colonization of modernity (the oppression of life itself by the powers of  government and economics) that peace and justice are the enemies of evangelism and mission. Much of our research reveals this either/or logic, logic that witnesses so powerfully to being caught up in the culture wars of modernity. Whether conservative or liberal, too many congregational and denominational leaders sit in the back of the room in my initial presentations to see on which side of the culture wars PMC falls.

At the first mention of powers and principalities, or extended periods of time in Dwelling in the Word, prayer, and spiritual discernment, most think they have their answer. The conservatives believe I have passed the first litmus test and the liberals begin to leave, if they have even shown up. At the first mention of racism, sexism, and classism as primary examples of powers and principalities, many of the conservatives join them. When I start suggesting we have turned peace and justice into idols, substitutes for the reign of God, rather than gifts of God, the remaining liberals feel free, even morally obligated, to leave.

I shall never forget a gross example of this phenomenon. Soon after my book *Welcoming the Stranger* was published, I was invited by the campus pastors of a major mainline denomination to speak about the book at their yearly retreat. They were known as a thoughtful, well-read group who were working in a tough but critical location in the modern world. Since I deeply believe the church is a truth-seeking community and that we have too often in the modern era given up that primal task to the universities that we once founded and funded, I wanted to be with these critical thought-leaders and seekers of truth. I was delighted.

Then the retreat leaders learned that their other preferred speaker, a well-known spiritual writer of the liberal persuasion, could not attend. Incidentally, it was my first clue that choosing to write a book with a subtitle including the word evangelism made me a conservative.

This other speaker also had written about Christian hospitality. I had read his work with appreciation and had included it in my own work, but I found his understanding thoroughly caught up in what I, following my teacher Wayne Booth, call the modern dogma. He fully privatized the practice of Christian hospitality while tying it to peace and justice, an appropriate connection made painfully unpersuasive given his understanding of intimacy and hospitality.

The group decided they needed to make sure his view was heard and that they did not want me to respond directly to his concept of hospitality since he would not be there to defend it. Their solution was to publish a guide to the event with chosen passages from his work on hospitality and, then, an outline of what they wanted to hear from me!

Never, I repeat, never have I experienced, before or since, a higher need to control what I would say to a group of gathered Christians. They literally spelled out in a paragraph following each of his paragraphs in each session of the retreat what they wanted to hear from me.

I called an executive in the organization whom I had known for a number of years for advice. He said he would look into the process and get back to me. He indicated in his follow-up that I had not misunderstood their desire. He explained on their behalf that they had had several very contentious retreats where conversations between speakers had divided them and created a very negative atmosphere, and they wanted to avoid this kind of conflict. Frankly, I had heard of this pattern and shared their desire to avoid it. As long as they perceived the conversation within the terms of modern culture wars, however, I feared it would be hard to get a hearing. I offered to withdraw without comment. They demurred. I suspect it was getting too late and they were quite confident I would know my place.

The event took place. Their defensiveness was patent but in most cases civil. I experienced the usual ritual attacks on conservatism—I genuinely share those criticisms—and some had known of my ministry in multicultural settings and my long-standing commitment to issues of peace and justice. Most were confused but preferred to stay in the terms of culture wars. One, in his candid critique of the time together, admitted that for the first time in his ministry he imagined being able to hear the "E" word without desiring to leave the room. (At the time, conservatives in the general political environment were on the ascendancy and the "L" word, liberal, was under attack. One could appreciate his somewhat reactionary defensiveness.) Among his peers in the room and in the leadership of his denomination he had little grounds to fear for his liberalism.

One of many things this incident taught me was that among very thoughtful, well-read, university-located ministers in this denomination, little recognition of the colonization of modern culture was present. Indeed, the rather unreflective power of modernity's colonization was well in place, and my association of evangelism, peace, and justice in a seamless conversation was simply too discordant to the imaginations of most of this group.

PMC is designed to wake up its participants from the modern drowsiness and tranquilization of Christian sensibilities, wake up to witness to the reign of God. PMC invites, cajoles, presses, even begs them to wake up and reject this oppression.

To my delight, by the Learning and Growing Phase in the PMC

spiritual journey, most participants begin to set aside culture wars as a means of evaluating how they spend their time and with whom they spend it. By this time, enough leaders have woken up and begun to do their own spiritual discernment and critical theology. They have found in their own local church and its surrounding environment, among the other churches in their cluster, and among their other missional partners the life-giving alternative of discerning God's preferred and promised future and, to the best of their abilities, are learning and growing into that future. They see that evangelism is simply their intentional actions to initiate persons into the reign of God. They see that these intentional actions take place within loving and trustworthy relationships and follow from their own waking up to witness the reign of God in their own lives rather than from some set of techniques to manipulate people to share their beliefs and values. The contrast is profound, and so are the results.

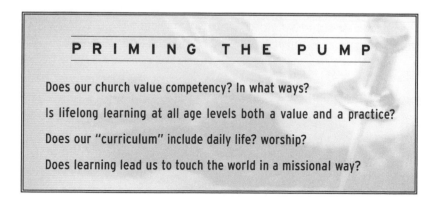

PRIMING THE PUMP

Does our church value competency? In what ways?

Is lifelong learning at all age levels both a value and a practice?

Does our "curriculum" include daily life? worship?

Does learning lead us to touch the world in a missional way?

SHARING AND MENTORING

THE LAST FEW CHAPTERS have followed what appears to be a linear development, the four phases of the PMC spiritual journey. Of course, spiritual journeys do not follow simple linear developments, and the model of change proposed in PMC precisely refuses to imagine that it is simply a matter of putting together a series of events, filled with workshops and lectures on new things to do, that will inevitably lead your congregation from the maintenance of Christendom into the New Missional Era. By now you know how unlikely those results would be. Quite to the contrary, we imagine the entire journey quite differently.

We imagine each local church as a sailboat, large, small, or in-between, that has for a long time been part of a great armada sailing within the sight of land on well-traveled routes. Now, for various reasons, a great spiritual tsunami has blown the armada apart and put these sailboats on shore in various states of dishevelment and destruction.

We have invited your sailboat to join a small cluster of other sailboats setting out into uncharted waters with only a promised goal on the horizon and a clear sense that the necessary gifts and capacities for this journey are present in the crew and will be provided along the way in a just-in-time pattern.

We try to teach the basic spiritual practices for sailing the Holy Gust and give some buoys for each sailboat to pass on our mutual journey. We provide guidance on the basis of years of assisting such journeys and our belief that the Triune God grants all the gifts and capacities necessary to achieve God's preferred and promised future.

While each congregation's crew engages these spiritual practices, we provide mentoring and are looking for additional mentors. We trust that congregations will learn more from one another than they will learn from us. Unfortunately, we have learned that congregations seldom, if ever, learn from one another without this intentional clustering. If they did, they would be regularly seeking to learn from one another on their own.

We have learned that we can, thanks be to God, broker their learning from one another. We can midwife the new life waiting to be born in them. We can create safe, innovative practices of acting and reflecting that coach and mentor these congregations and their crews into finding their missional vocation and learning and growing into it.

This final chapter describes some of the ways this sharing and mentoring takes place. Over the years, we have committed ourselves to "innovating your church's capacities to be renewed in mission"

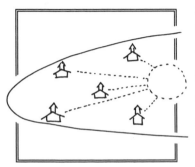

rather than replacing your capacities. This commitment presumes we will work ourselves out of a job and leave in place those who will mentor and share, midwife and guide the next generation of congregations into the PMC spiritual journey.

Sharing and mentoring take place through relationships. The relationships begin with the earliest connections between partners who call and speak with us and then multiply as the Spirit creates them.

THE SYSTEMS APPROACH

Within a theological and spiritual framework, we use a systems approach to understanding culture and organizations. Over the years we have learned that for sustained innovation it is not enough to work with one congregation at a time. Although early prejudices and research suggested this one-congregation-at-a-time model, we confused a number of research findings with the conclusion that we should work only with congregations.

The findings suggested that congregations were the primary social agents for changing congregations. This remains true. According to the work of Lesslie Newbigin and his students in the Gospel and Our Culture Network, congregations are the chief social agent of missional church. However, congregations can 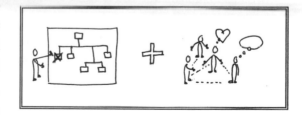 learn much more and innovate more efficiently, effectively, and faithfully when they work with other congregations struggling to do the same things.

But this rarely happens. The pattern remains a show-and-tell format, even from some of the most famous teaching congregations. They spend most of their time at their conferences showing and telling how they do what they do. Some actually know what they are doing; most have been ingenious, inspired, even brilliant, but instinctual local leaders seldom reflect enough to learn the principles and patterns that might be useful in other social and cultural settings and settle for showing and telling their own practices and decision-making patterns.

Even those who know what they have done and are able to critically evaluate those patterns tend not to know how to share those critical insights with leaders from other congregations who are in very different cultural and social circumstances. Even more significantly, they seldom sustain long-term coaching and mentoring relationships beyond consulting visits, visits that involve significant travel and expenses. These more sophisticated teaching congregations could make a very big difference in the New Missional Era. I remain hopeful for their roles.

Recently, we have spent a good deal of time learning from the emergent church movement. These congregations have sought to move beyond the modernist models of church growth technology and quick-fix techniques. They have found new and exciting niches for developing Christian community. Our consultants have enjoyed getting to know their leaders and learning from their innovating ministries. They represent a very important worldwide resource for innovating missional church. I had the chance to help facilitate, with Alan Roxburgh, an international gathering of emergent church leaders. I personally have visited a number of these congregations and have become friends with their leaders. In particular, I have been influenced by the works of Brian McLaren, Tim Keel, Steve Taylor, Andrew Menzies, and Karen Ward. From the place of the congregation, they are providing truly innovative models of missional church. May their numbers multiply.

Still, a purely congregational approach, or a purely congregational-based teaching model, does not sufficiently reflect a Trinitarian ecclesiology or recognize the role of complex systems that can, do, and could more effectively innovate missional church. Congregations are, of course, systems in themselves. They also participate in diverse and complex systems, and such a systems approach shapes PMC.

Without going into an extensive discussion of systems theories, we generally use two broad categories of systems in PMC: closed systems and open systems. Their names go a long way in describing them.

CLOSED SYSTEMS

Closed systems are close-knit, focus on the sociology of belonging, and require extremely high boundaries either to join or to leave. The classic closed system is the family.

In the past several decades, family systems theory has profitably been used to understand church life, especially congregational life. Naming just a few of the concepts will illustrate my point:

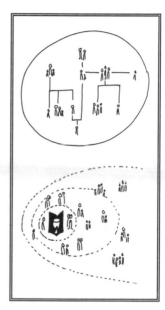

1. *The principle of the designated patient underlines system over individual. The designated patient might be the person sent to the therapist because he or she is acting out, but in systems theory that person represents more a symptom of a dysfunctional family than the real source of the trouble.*

2. *The concept of dynamic homeostasis explains how personnel may change and organizational structure may change but systems tend to remain unchanged (homeostatic) even though they appear quite dynamic.*

3. *The powerful insights into birth order and patterns of accountability with parents and siblings make a huge difference in understanding authority structures in congregations.*

The list could go on. These and other basic concepts borrowed from family systems and other closed systems theories provide a critical analytic and diagnostic tool when working with congregations. They add rich insight into leadership development at several stages of PMC. They fall easily into place with congregations because it is common to understand congregations as private space and to use the metaphor of family for naming the dynamics of a congregation. And, as a metaphor, family has its place since it does describe some of the powerful dynamics of a typical congregation.

OPEN SYSTEMS

It is extremely important to understand the use of the word family as a metaphor when understanding a congregation; that is, it is and is not the character of a congregation to be a family, to have characteristics of a closed system. One of the critical reasons many congregations die follows from mistaking family as metaphor for family as literal. Healthy congregations are not families; they are open systems.

Open systems focus on joining and belonging sociology. They have permeable boundaries rather than the high boundaries of closed systems. Open systems expect, facilitate, and organize themselves to allow people to join them and provide for belonging with boundaries that are considerably lower than those of a family.

Even though family systems theory can help diagnose dysfunction and help individuals within the system gain self-definition and other healthy skills, family systems theory cannot provide the most applicable analogies for growing, healthy congregations. PMC uses an open systems approach to frame our use of closed systems analysis and training.

PMC RELATIONSHIPS

PMC CONSULTANTS

Whenever possible, we use teams of two consultants in all our work at Church Innovations. We have learned that there is deep wisdom in this pattern that grows out of Jesus' own practice of sending his disciples out two by two, as pairs, "to every town and place where he himself intended to go" (Luke 10:1). Indeed, we can see a pattern of multiplication through partnering. Partnering also recognizes the inherent need in every individual to receive mutual support and balance.

The primary PMC consultant maintains the relationship with the cluster and the systems leaders (often judicatory staff) who are working with the cluster of congregations. The primary consultant is the chief connection between the Church Innovations team and the systems and cluster leadership team. Most of the coaching of systems team leaders takes place through the primary consultant. This consultant aims at developing a designated member of the systems team (usually a judicatory staff person) to become a partner with

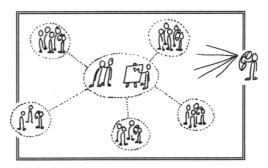

him or her in a subsequent cluster. This is a critical part of "innovating your church's capacities . . ." This relationship between the judicatory leader and the primary PMC consultant oversees the innovation of capacities of the system itself.

PMC consultant teams lead most of the early cluster events. Aside from worship and logistical details, it is the PMC consultant team that facilitates, teaches, coaches, and mentors congregational leaders. Over time and at the encouragement of the PMC primary consultant, members of the systems team begin to play greater roles in later cluster events. The goal in this process is to develop a team of leaders who can recruit and start a second, third, fourth cluster in their judicatory.

PMC TRAINERS

Each cluster event has specific things to be shared. In the first cluster event there is a lot of information about the process and the basic spiritual practices for the PMC spiritual journey. In that event, specific training needs to be done with pastors/ministers, Steering Team members, and the Listening Leaders. One Church Innovations team member in attendance at each event is specifically experienced at carrying out that training. PMC trainers may also function as PMC consultants, but they move from cluster to cluster in their area of expertise while the primary consultant is a consistent part of the cluster.

PMC PHONE LOOP

In our first years of doing this work, we made a very important discovery: the phone loop. We found that an every-other-month phone call from one of our staff persons to a key leader, often the pastor/minister of the congregation, was a critical part of the forward movement for the congregation.

Our phone loop staff is headed by a certified, trained, and experienced spiritual director. Other members of the phone loop staff 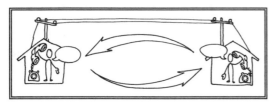 have the gifts of spiritual direction, and many have been new church developers, redevelopers, or exceptionally strong leaders in PMC congregations.

During the phone loop conversation, which is confidential, the pastor/minister prays with the spiritual director and shares how the spiritual journey is going. The phone loop spiritual director may share general patterns and concerns with the Church Innovations PMC team but never will report who said what.

Pastor/ministers have found this phone loop extremely valuable, giving it very high marks in their evaluations and reflections on PMC. One of the important reasons for its value is that contemporary church leaders find it very hard to find the time to engage in regular and sustained spiritual practices. Too much of their time gets filled with preparing sermons, Bible classes, other Christian education, community organizing, conflict resolution, visitation, and administration. Worse, most feel considerable guilt regarding this failure and do not seek out assistance and accountability.

The pastor/minister day at each cluster event is designed to give basic training for leading the PMC spiritual journey in the local church. PMC takes very seriously the notion that this spiritual journey must begin with the pastor/minister. Major pieces of the early work in these cluster events are given over to basic spiritual practices. The phone loop follows up, supports, and encourages these important practices.

MENTORS & ASYMMETRICAL PARTNERING

From the first time the Church Innovations PMC team starts to interact with members of the systems team, judicatory staff, and congregational leadership, they are looking for and finding mentors. Mentors are persons who already understand the basic PMC principles or who readily pick up on them and have the gifts to share them in a nonthreatening way with others. Mentors become a critical piece of the brokering of congregations to one another.

One of the great and interesting challenges of PMC clusters is asymmetrical partnering. By asymmetrical partnering, I mean the creation of partnering between congregations and groups that have very different resources and social settings. The obvious form is the gross difference between the amounts of fiscal and material resources available to congregations. In international work, we find the same set of challenges in even more clearer relief.

Very early on we saw this as a marvelous opportunity to help congregations begin to partner with one another rather than wait for the external system to solve the problem by simply bringing money to the table. All the congregations involved would need to negotiate with one another about jointly finding the financial resources for paying for PMC participation.

These negotiations were not necessarily pleasant or easy. In modernity it is easier to talk about sex and politics than money. This is especially true in the church, where somehow we have accepted the modern assumption that polite people do not talk about money in public.

In such conversations, we encourage the group to go beyond the usual solution of modernity that says the easiest way to partner is through the great equalizer of legal tender, cash. Of course, for all sorts of good reasons the dominant economy depends upon the liquidity of value that cash represents. However, we encourage the group to move beyond this solution to asymmetrical partnering.

Asymmetrical partnering includes cash but also looks at various other values that might be included in the partnering. Diversity, especially the experience of successful engagement and flourishing in diversity, is seldom valued enough in the wider world, but in the church it is a deeply-held value. Of course, there are congregations in every economic and cultural setting that can complain vociferously about someone else excluding them, but they have been unable to effectively, efficiently, and faithfully diversify themselves.

Asymmetrical partnering depends upon honest talk about money and the values we use it to express. A kind of bartering is the result—bartering that makes possible honest conversation, tough accountability, and grows out of and affirms a shared sense of meaning, mission, and purpose.

I remember seeing a long-term relationship develop between two congregations that might have been unlikely except for two mentors, one from each of the congregations, who began working together with their own congregations and eventually with others. One congregation was in Simi Valley, Calif., north of Los Angeles, just down the road from Ronald Reagan's last resting place and Presidential Library. The other congregation was in south-central Los Angeles. Needless to say, the cultural and class differences between the congregations and their geography had not brought them together before.

Through PMC they chose to be in the same cluster. They sought to cross some of those boundaries. From among them came two extraordinary mentors: Maria and Mark (not their real names). Maria worked as an RN administrator in a hospital and understood in-service training across diverse social boundaries. Mark was a professional strategic planner for a major aerospace corporation. As the cluster meetings began, they ended up as a dyad in Dwelling in the Word. Out of that situation, they began to feel freer to share some of their hopes and hurts. They also were very effective communicators and leaders in their own Steering Teams.

In the case of these two congregations, there was a huge difference in the amount of cash available. Neither had much volunteer time to offer, but they were able to see that by teaming Maria and Mark, they could barter with one another and eventually with other congregations to work together at planning and diversity. I sat in on a couple  of their coaching/consulting times with congregations and wished that I could multiply them. They were invaluable to the cluster, to their own congregations, and eventually to dozens of other congregations in the Los Angeles area.

PMC SUMMER MISSIONAL INSTITUTE

Mentoring takes very different forms and involves a variety of personalities and gifts. To make this delightful plenitude of diversity work with the PMC spiritual journey, however, we attempt to keep everyone on the same clear path. Needless to say, the PMC spiritual journey has many components and requires a rather high degree of awareness and commitment to missional church theology and practices. Without this awareness and commitment, these mentoring gifts can do great harm. Unfortunately, we have found this to be the case time and time again.

We have, as a result, begun to invite mentors and other leaders in the clusters and other parts of the system to join us at our Summer Missional Institute and other training events that are separate from the cluster events. During these PMC Institute events we bring together key leaders in the PMC movement from around the world. This allows for tremendous cross-fertilization, playful and serendipitous insights and ideas, international friendships, and innovates PMC capacities.

In all these ways, through all these relationships, we try to increase the capacities of churches to be renewed in mission. We believe that over these past decades God has blessed this work and made possible its continued growth. We pray that by the power of the Holy Spirit it will effectively, efficiently, and faithfully continue to do so.

PRIMING THE PUMP

Given our immersion in cultural transformation to be and do "missional church," how competent do we feel?

Are we competent enough to keep up the momentum? to raise up and form the next generation? to trust and work the process?

Again, where would we place our X on the missional map?

Given our failures and successes, what words of wisdom can we harvest now?

Epilogue:
Is all this necessary?

At a Summer Missional Institute session, a denominational leader who was new to missional church and PMC, but clearly open to the process of spiritual discernment, asked as his last question, "Is all this necessary? It's so complex."

PMC seems complex to the beginner and even to those of us who work at it all the time. PMC seems too much, especially if you are convinced that the challenges facing the church in our time really are not especially greater than the challenges faced in earlier decades of the 20th century. PMC is too much if technical change can attend to the contemporary challenge. If you believe that simply reorganizing the local church or denominational structures is an effective, efficient, and faithful response to contemporary challenges, PMC simply is not for you. PMC for you would be a nightmare.

If, however, you were able to identify with the opening chapter in any basic way, PMC is for you. If you could say with that chapter, "We are here now," then adaptive change is required. Even the Missional Engagement Teams that address adaptive challenges will not be enough without discovering and putting into place the partners for innovating missional church in the Discovery Phase. Even if you have successful outcomes to your Missional Engagement Teams, without a shared missional vocation, a compelling sense of missional call, and a plan to embody it, those successful experiments will not multiply and transform your local church. Without establishing a learning organization, the local church and the parts of the system that support it will soon be caught in the contemporary fast-forward change.

Still, is PMC all that complex? Certainly nothing in the journey of spiritual discernment is rocket science or utterly new; indeed, we have tried to avoid such things. PMC in many ways is simply getting back to basics, the core practices of forming Christian community. These were the basics before the Christian community took on the responsibility of maintaining Western culture. These basics depend upon discovering our partners, relying on the Holy Spirit alive and well in these partners, and risking new ways of doing the same old task of forming Christian community. In this very simple sense, PMC is the basics, and we are here now, at the point in church history for getting back to the basics.

SELECTED BIBLIOGRAPHY

THE RESOURCES LISTED in this bibliography provide some of the theoretical basis for this much more practical book. I have created a short list of books from the complete bibliography for readers taking their first steps. For anyone who wants to go deeper— in some cases, much deeper—the voices on the second list will help you understand the basic framework for *We Are Here Now*.

FIRST STEPS

Barrett, Lois, ed. *Treasure in Clay Jars: Patterns in Missional Faithfulness*. The Gospel and Our Culture Series. Grand Rapids, Mich.: Wm. B. Eerdmans Publishing Co., 2004.

Block, Peter. *Flawless Consulting: A Guide to Getting Your Expertise Used*. San Francisco: Jossey-Bass/Pfeiffer, 2000.

Branson, Mark Lau. *Memories, Hopes, and Conversations: Appreciative Inquiry and Congregational Change*. Herndon, Va.: Alban Institute, 2004.

Hadaway, C. Kirk. *Behold I Do a New Thing: Transforming Communities of Faith*. Cleveland: Pilgrim Press, 2001.

Heifetz, Ronald A., and Marty Linsky. *Leadership on the Line*. Boston: Harvard Business School Press, 2002.

Lakoff G., and M. Johnson. *Metaphors We Live By*. Chicago: University of Chicago Press, 1980.

Mead, Loren B. *The Once and Future Church: Reinventing the Congregation for a New Mission Frontier*. Herndon, Va.: Alban Institute, 1991.

GOING DEEPER

Ammerman, Nancy Tatom, and Arthur Emery Farnsley. *Congregation & Community*. 5th ed. New Brunswick, N.J.: Rutgers University Press, 2003.

Barrett, Lois, ed. *Treasure in Clay Jars: Patterns in Missional Faithfulness*. The Gospel and Our Culture Series. Grand Rapids, Mich.: Wm. B. Eerdmans Publishing Co., 2004.

Best, Steven, and Douglas Kellner. *The Postmodern Turn*. New York: Guilford Press, 1997.

Bevans, Stephen B. *Models of Contextual Theology*. Rev. and exp. ed. Faith and Cultures Series. Maryknoll, N.Y.: Orbis Books, 2002.

Block, Peter. *Flawless Consulting: A Guide to Getting Your Expertise Used*. San Francisco: Jossey-Bass/Pfeiffer, 2000.

Booth, Wayne C. *The Modern Dogma and the Rhetoric of Assent.* Notre Dame: University of Notre Dame Press, 1974.

Bosch, David Jacobus. *Transforming Mission: Paradigm Shifts in Theology of Mission.* American Society of Missiology Series, no. 16. Maryknoll, N.Y.: Orbis Books, 1991.

Branson, Mark Lau. *Memories, Hopes, and Conversations: Appreciative Inquiry and Congregational Change.* Herndon, Va.: Alban Institute, 2004.

Brownson, James V., et al. *StormFront: The Good News of God.* Grand Rapids, Mich.: Wm. B. Eerdmans Publishing Co., 2003.

Callahan, Kennon. *Strong, Small Congregations: Creating Strengths and Health for Your Congregation.* San Francisco: Jossey-Bass, 2000.

Cladis, George. *Leading the Team-Based Church: How Pastors and Church Staffs Can Grow Together into a Powerful Fellowship of Leaders.* San Francisco: Jossey-Bass, 1999.

Coalter, Milton J., John M. Mulder, and Louis Weeks. *Vital Signs: The Promise of Mainstream Protestantism.* Grand Rapids, Mich.: Wm. B. Eerdmans Publishing Co., 2002.

Dobbert, Marion L. *Ethnographic Research.* New York: Praeger Publications, 1982.

Finke, Roger, and Rodney Stark. *The Churching of America, 1776–1990: Winners and Losers in Our Religious Economy.* New Brunswick, N.J.: Rutgers University Press, 1992.

Granberg-Michaelson, Wesley. *Leadership from Inside Out: Spirituality and Organizational Change.* New York: Crossroad Publishing, 2004.

Guder, Darrell L., ed. *Missional Church: A Vision for the Sending of the Church in North America.* The Gospel and Our Culture Series. Grand Rapids, Mich.: Wm. B. Eerdmans Publishing Co., 1998.

Hadaway, C. Kirk. *Behold I Do a New Thing: Transforming Communities of Faith.* Cleveland: Pilgrim Press, 2001.

Hatch, Mary Jo. *Organization Theory: Modern, Symbolic, and Postmodern Perspectives.* Oxford, N.Y.: Oxford University Press, 1997.

Hatch, Nathan O. *The Democratization of American Christianity.* New Haven: Yale University Press, 1989.

Heifetz, Ronald A. *Leadership without Easy Answers.* Cambridge, Mass.: Belknap Press of Harvard University Press, 1994.

Heifetz, Ronald A., and Marty Linsky. *Leadership on the Line.* Boston: Harvard Business School Press, 2002.

Hunsberger, George R., and Craig Van Gelder. *The Church between Gospel and Culture: The Emerging Mission in North America.* Grand Rapids, Mich.: Wm. B. Eerdmans Publishing Co., 1996.

Jenkins, Philip. *The Next Christendom: The Coming of Global Christianity.* Oxford, N.Y.: Oxford University Press, 2002.

Keifert, Patrick R. *Testing the Spirits: Congregations as Schools of Mission and Theology.* Grand Rapids, Mich.: Wm. B. Eerdmans Publishing Co., 2006.

———. *Welcoming the Stranger: A Public Theology of Worship and Evangelism.* Minneapolis: Fortress Press, 1992.

Keifert, Patrick R., and Alan Padgett. *But Is It All True: The Bible and the Question of Truth*. Grand Rapids, Mich.: Wm. B. Eerdmans Pubishing Co., 2006.

Kelsey, David H. *To Understand God Truly: What's Theological about a Theological School*. Louisville: Westminster/John Knox Press, 1992.

Lakoff, G., and M. Johnson. *Metaphors We Live By*. Chicago: University of Chicago Press, 1980.

Laszlo, Ervin. *The Systems View of the World: A Holistic Vision for Our Time, Advances in Systems Theory, Complexity, and the Human Sciences*. Cresskill, N.J.: Hampton Press, 1996.

Mead, Loren B. *The Once and Future Church: Reinventing the Congregation for a New Mission Frontier*. Herndon, Va.: Alban Institute, 1991.

Mullin, Robert Bruce, and Russell E. Richey, eds. *Reimagining Denominationalism: Interpretive Essays*. Religion in America Series. New York: Oxford University Press, 1994.

Newbigin, Lesslie. *Foolishness to the Greeks: The Gospel and Western Culture*. Grand Rapids, Mich.: Wm. B. Eerdmans Publishing Co., 1986.

———. *The Gospel in a Pluralist Society*. Grand Rapids, Mich.: Wm. B. Eerdmans Publishing Co., 1989.

Olsen, Charles M. *Transforming Church Boards into Communities of Spiritual Leaders*. Herndon, Va.: Alban Institute, 1995.

Pascale, Richard T., Mark Milleman, and Linda Gioja. *Surfing the Edge of Chaos: The Laws of Nature and the New Laws of Business*. 1st ed. New York: Crown Business, 2000.

Regele, Mike. *Robust Church Development: A Vision for Mobilizing Regional Bodies in Support of Missional Congregations*. Cincinnati, Ohio: Percept Group, Inc. 2003.

Ricoeur, Paul. *The Rule of Metaphor*. Toronto: University of Toronto Press, 1977.

———. *Time and Narrative*. 3 vols. Chicago: University of Chicago Press, 1984, 1985, 1988.

Rogers, Everett M. *Diffusion of Innovations*. New York: Free Press of Glencoe, 1962.

Roxburgh, Alan. *The Sky Is Falling: Leaders Lost in Transition*. Eagle, Idaho: Allelon Publishing, 2005.

Sanneh, Lamin O. *Translating the Message: The Missionary Impact on Culture*. American Society of Missiology Series, no. 13. Maryknoll, N.Y.: Orbis Books, 1989.

Schein, Edgar H. *Organizational Culture and Leadership*. San Francisco: Jossey-Bass, 2004.

Schmemann, Alexander. *For the Life of the World*. New York: National Student Christian Federation, 1963.

Schreiter, Robert J. *Constructing Local Theologies*. Maryknoll, N.Y.: Orbis Books, 1985.

Senge, Peter M. *The Fifth Discipline: The Art and Practice of the Learning Organization*. New York: DoubleDay, 1990.

Simpson, Gary M. *Critical Social Theory: Prophetic Reason, Civil Society, and Christian Imagination*. Guides to Theological Inquiry Series. Minneapolis: Fortress Press, 2002.

Stark, Rodney, *The Rise of Christianity: How the Obscure, Marginal Jesus Movement Became the Dominant Religious Force in the Western World in a Few Centuries.* San Francisco: HarperSanFrancisco, 1997.

Terry, Robert W. *Authentic Leadership: Courage in Action.* San Francisco: Jossey-Bass, 1993.

———. Seven *Zones for Leadership: Acting Authentically in Stability and Chaos.* Palo Alto, Calif.: Davies-Black Pub., 2001.

Textor, Robert B. *Handbook on Ethnographic Futures Research,* 3rd ed. Stanford: Stanford University Press, 1980.

Van Gelder, Craig. "Postmodernism and Evangelicals: A Unique Missiological Challenge at the Beginning of the Twenty-First Century." *Missiology: An International Review* 30, no. 4 (2002): 491–504.

Van Manen, Max. *Researching Lived Experience.* New York: State University of New York Press, 1990.

Volf, Miroslav. *After Our Likeness: The Church as the Image of the Trinity, Sacra Doctrina.* Grand Rapids, Mich: Wm. B. Eerdmans Publishing Co., 1998.

Walls, Andrew F. *The Missionary Movement in Christian History: Studies in the Transmission of Faith.* Maryknoll, N.Y.: Orbis Books, 1996.

Wind, James P., and James Welborn Lewis. *American Congregations.* 2 vols. Chicago: University of Chicago Press, 1994.

Welker, Michael. *God the Spirit.* Translated by John F. Hoffmeyer. Minneapolis: Fortress Press, 1994.

Zizioulas, John. *Being as Communion: Studies in Personhood and the Church.* Contemporary Greek Theologians Series, no. 4. Crestwood, N.Y.: St. Vladimir's Seminary Press, 1985.

GLOSSARY

Action/Reflection Learning: The primary model of learning used in PMC.

We practice a set of actions (listening, for example) and then reflect on what we have learned. This model follows from the assumption that adult learners learn what they want to learn, not what we want to teach them. It also focuses on learning from experience with the aid of other sources, including theory and research, rather than starting with theories and research and trying to apply them.

Adaptive vs. Technical Change: A major distinction used in the PMC spiritual journey that underlines and distinguishes the importance of both types of change.

Adaptive change involves a change of culture requiring knowledge, skills, and practices we do not have at this point or have not found and put together as an effective force for change. Technical change involves change of organization and structure requiring knowledge, skills, and practices we do have or can find easily to put together as an effective force for change. The New Missional Era requires both.

Applied Ethnography: A form of ethnography, the writing of a culture, from the point of view of those within the culture.

The particular form we use (see Congregational Discovery) follows a decades-long development of ethnography used to support identity formation and change in local communities. Its use lessens the negative effects of introducing organizational change in a local culture.

Apostolic Age: *Roughly the years following Jesus' Ascension to the adoption of Christianity as one of the legal religions of the Roman Empire (313 A.D.) and the Fall of Rome (410 A.D.).*

Most importantly for this book, the focus was upon the formation of Christian community in the activity of joining the mission of God, the explicit witness to Jesus Christ. Increasingly after this period, in the face of tremendous transformation and destruction of the Graeco-Roman empire, the church also took on the business of maintaining Western culture. The melding of these two tasks created Christendom.

Catechumenate: *A process (and the people involved in it) for becoming Christian.*

In the Apostolic Age, the church offered persons who were seekers and inquirers regarding Jesus and the Christian faith a deliberate ritual process for ordering their last stages of preparing for baptism and life within the Christian community. Once inquirers or seekers entered this process, they were called Catechumens. The persons who guided their journey were called Catechists. The summary of what these Catechists taught was often put into the form of questions and answers called a Catechism. The New Missional Era is well-served by local churches who form as a central part of their life a contemporary form of the Catechumenate.

Christendom: *An often-used term with several common meanings.*

The general meaning is the rule of Christ or Christianity. In the PMC process, it refers to a particular period in the Latin Church, the church of the European West, that began to form in 400 A.D. and continued in various forms into the modern period. It grew in strength from the beginning of the Holy Roman Empire (800

A.D.) through the Reformation, and began to lose its strong influence on government in the 17th and 18th centuries, a process that has continued to this day. With the separation of Church and State and the disestablishment of "folks church" Christianity, many have named the present period Post-Christendom. In this book, the practical effect of this recent loss of influence profoundly changes the relationship between the local church and its immediate environment. In this new Era, the local church can no longer assume that the immediate environment of family, friends, co-workers, work, school, and civil society provide the necessary social practices to encourage the formation of Christian community. As a result, congregations can flourish only if they provide those basic practices of forming Christian community. This is a core concept of Missional Church.

Civil Society: *The various organizations that make up the space in modern society between the private realm and the State.*

Some of this space has formal organizations like Boy Scouts and the Red Cross, but most of it is made up of much more ad hoc associations that carry out diverse, influential purposes in the public space of our local and national communities.

Congregational Discovery: *One of the practices in the first phase of PMC, Discovery.*

We have found over the years that congregations really do not know what they know about themselves, their own culture and identity. This discovery process invites them to disciplined listening to themselves, their immediate community, within the frame of the Biblical narrative. In PMC, we accomplish this listening by means of Listening Leaders, members of the congregation who gather and create a collection of stories and assist in interpreting them to better understand the congregation's narrative.

Critical Theory: *A method for reading and understanding the picture of the local culture, as gathered by members of the culture itself.*

In PMC we read the local culture's self-understanding in terms of certain wider patterns of human relations and interest. Bringing this "critical perspective" helps congregation members attend to questions of justice and economics from a Christian perspective. Habits such as Dwelling in the Word and corporate spiritual discernment provoke critical engagement with the powers and principalities, sin, death, and evil at work in how we live with one another.

Diffusion of Innovation: *A model of change acknowledging the present challenge facing most churches is adaptive rather than simply organizational change.*

The Diffusion of Innovation model grows out of substantial discussion of cultural change coming from experience of Western culture's attempts to introduce organizational change in non-Western cultures, only to find that such interventions are usually harmful and fail. PMC draws upon the wisdom of this discussion of cultural change, including but not limited to the work of Everett Rogers. It includes models of Applied Ethnography, Critical Theory, and Hermeneutics developed to explain the diffusion of innovation in cross-cultural settings. In PMC, all change comes into being within a process of spiritual discernment and theological reflection, a genuine seeking to understand God truly and act into God's preferred and promised future.

Disestablishment of Church: *A term noting the effect of three major changes in the relationship between church and culture in the United States leaving the church with less general social influence than it once enjoyed.*

The initial disestablishment formally begins with the First Amendment's disallowing a State-established church. The second moment of disestablishment comes with the emigration of large numbers of Roman Catholics. The third moment comes following World War II with the increasing place and influence of Judaism, Islam, and other traditional and world-wide religions.

Dwelling in the Word: *A practice of a group of people listening to the Word of God, usually in relatively short chunks of the Bible, over long periods of time.*

This practice asks participants to attend and assert through a double listening process—first listening to the Scripture, then listening "a reasonably friendly-looking stranger into free speech" on what they heard from that same Scripture. Then participants assert to a larger group what one heard from the reasonably friendly-looking stranger. By regular repetition, this practice becomes a habit of forming Christian community within the Word of God and forming our decision and actions within the biblical narrative.

Fact-Value Split: *The modern belief that all of human knowing and experience is divided between facts and values—a very small number of facts and an almost infinite number of values.*

The facts derive from objective, reasonable, public methods. The values derive from relative, even subjective, irrational but profound values. With this split, faith is more often than not relegated to the private, irrational but profound sphere of life. While previous traditions allowed for a distinction between the private and public, the modern period created a separation of the two, both in time and space.

Gap Theory of Change: *A model of change focusing on the use of some external evaluative tool, supposedly universally applicable to local churches, that establishes a baseline evaluation.*

Once the baseline is established, a planning and visioning process establishes a future point in time (usually three to five years) where these universally established objectives and characteristics of the local church will be stronger. The Gap is between the first evaluation and the second future success point. The purpose is to focus attention of the local church on filling this gap in a planned and purposeful way. PMC values this model of change, essentially an organizational model, to address discrete technical changes as a part of a larger cultural model of innovating missional church.

Gospel and Our Culture Network (GOCN): *A loose association of people and organizations in North America joined to a conversation resulting from the work of Lesslie Newbigin and encouraged by him.*

This North American network had/has roughly equivalent conversations in the United Kingdom, Australia, New Zealand, and South Africa.

Judicatory: *A most unhappy term.*

We are looking for a better one to name the various forms of association, fellowship, and sometimes systems of accountability that form a relatively close relationship among a group of local churches. The term smacks of Christendom, but it points to the reality that local churches do form such associations even if not in the traditional forms of diocese, conferences, synods, districts, regional bodies, etc. Despite earlier opinion on our part, we have learned that judicatories are critical parts of a system for both innovating missional church and also sustaining it. As one

Mennonite bishop noted: "Success without succession is failure." If we do not have an associational system for supporting local churches through good times and bad times, we often do not have a succession of missional local churches.

Hermeneutics: *A technical term for talking about the way we read and interpret texts and the world.*

In PMC, we use hermeneutics to attend to the assumptions that often work "behind our back" that nonetheless profoundly shape how we interpret the Scriptures and the world. We especially attend to the narratives and metaphors that deeply shape what we see, hear, and experience.

Managing Polarities: *A process that begins by distinguishing those challenges that represent problems to be solved or obstacles to be overcome from those challenges that remain a major part of the dynamics of a church system.*

Not all challenges are problems; indeed, some challenges are polarities that, if lessened or eliminated, actually lessen or eliminate the community. Like a battery that has two poles, positive and negative, if we lessen either pole, we lose the energy in the battery. If we eliminate the poles, the battery is dead. So, in church systems, we need to discern the poles that can enliven the system if we manage them wisely. This wise management requires spiritual discernment.

Missio Dei: *A Latin expression roughly translated "God's mission."*

The term became identified in ecumenical church circles in the latter half of the 20th century with a theology emphasizing the mission as God's—not primarily the churches'. This book assumes that the mission of God is far greater than the church, as the

Reign of God is greater than the church; however, the mission of God needs a church, among many other institutions, to carry out God's mission.

Missional Church: *A term used since the 19th Century and borrowed by the GOCN movement to emphasize that the Mission of God, while greater than the mission of the church, requires a church.*

A missional church focuses on being mission, not just doing mission. Missional church invites churches to move beyond being a spiritual gas station only providing spiritual services for individuals without forming them into Christian community. Missional church invites churches to move beyond forming a tight knit Christian community that cannot be porous and open to life among those who are not a part of their community. Missional church invites churches to engage with others in mission rather than sending persons or money elsewhere, avoiding this engagement.

Missional Engagement Team: *A significant relational group that tackles adaptive change challenges identified in the last part of Phase 1 and the first part of Phase 2.*

These Missional Engagement Teams reflect our partnership with the PMC Southern Africa and experiences in North America. The Teams focus on clarifying the adaptive challenge, more often than not misstated or misunderstood in the initial identification of adaptive challenges, and on innovating ways of meeting those challenges. Teams plunge into the community with whom their congregation seeks to be in mission to listen and learn. The Teams do not carry out the action they propose, though members of the Teams might well be invited to participate in embodying that action.

Missional Vocation: *The sense of calling and purpose a local church discerns through the journey of spiritual discernment in PMC.*

It is best stated in as short a description as possible making clear the difference between their particular local church and others. It answers the question: Having listened to the Word of God, ourselves, and our community, what part of God's mission in this place is our part of the action?

Modernity: *The period of European/American history (1650— 1950) that features the establishment of the modern Nation State, the disestablishment in various forms of the Church, the rise of the middle class, and the exponential growth of the influence of European/American culture throughout the world.*

Modernity especially noted the dominance of an epistemology (how we know) that tended to divide reality into facts and values.

New Missional Era: *A period of Church history recently created by the transformation of European/North American Christendom and the rise of a worldwide Christianity.*

When combined, these forces open a time and space for the church to learn from the deep wisdom of the first four centuries of Christianity, the lessons from the forming of Christendom, and the explosive energy of worldwide Christianity. The work of Lesslie Newbigin and David Bosch and their students helped define this new era.

Pastors/Ministers: *In the PMC spiritual journey, a general term referring to those persons or group of persons who are publicly accountable for the care and nurture of the local church.*

This includes a wide variety of offices or groups, depending upon the tradition of the Christian fellowship and associations.

Phases of the Partnership: *The spiritual discernment journey of PMC has four phases, four time periods, that focus the attention and action of the congregations and other leaders on four basic practices:*

(1) Discovering;

(2) Experimenting;

(3) Visioning for Embodiment; and

(4) Learning and Growing into patterns of Missional Church.

In each phase, the primary practice is to try out a set of actions and then reflect on what we learn and then try on another set of practices based upon those learnings.

Post-modern: *The period following Modernity that begins to question many of the primary assumptions of modern culture.*

More than a gathered culture and position, it represents a diversity of critical questions and explorations of modernity.

Significant Relational Groups: *Referring to various groups smaller than the local church as a whole that have as their primary practice the forming and sustaining of strong relationships amongst the members of the group.*

Sometimes this pattern is limited to "small" groups of 6-10; however, this reduction to one form of significant relational groups has often dominated the conversation in some circles of church renewal. PMC invites a larger definition that focuses on the basics of forming Christian community rather than specific organizational technologies or particular sizes of groups.

Worship Wars: *A popular expression referring to the intense conflict within churches trying to develop Christian worship appropriate for this transitional time between Christendom and the New Missional Era.*

Some churches became convinced that all forms of traditional Christian worship harmed the ability of the local church to reach out to seekers, inquirers, and many of their members. Many others saw this as a chance to strengthen those traditional forms of worship. Most are on a spectrum in between these two poles of the wars. In the local church, this has often led to conflict far more painful than even fights about sex and money.

PATRICK R. KEIFERT

Professor of Systematic Theology

Patrick Keifert was named an instructor in systematic theology at Luther Seminary in 1980 and was made associate professor in 1986, promoted to full professor in 1996. He has also been an adjunct professor at the School of Law, Hamline University, Saint Paul, MN since 1984.

His teaching experience began at Christ Seminary-Seminex where he was a teaching assistant in 1976-77 and instructor in systematic theology in the summer of 1980.

Ordained in 1978, Keifert served Pilgrim Evangelical Lutheran Church in Chicago (Interim, 1977-78; assistant pastor, 1978-1980); and was interim pastor at Lord of Life Lutheran Church, Renton, WA (Summer, 1982) and Trinity and Hope Lutheran Churches, Cody and Powell, WY (Summer 1983). He also served Galilee Lutheran Church, Roseville, MN in 1985.

Keifert is the President and Director of Research of Church Innovations Institute, a nonprofit organization dedicated to discovering and implementing tools for congregational renewal.

He has been the general editor of the Journal of Law and Religion, and served on the editorial boards of Word & World and Dialog.

He earned a B.A. degree in 1973 from Valparaiso (IN) University, where he was a Christ College Scholar, and an M. Div. Degree from Christ Seminary-Seminex in 1977. He received a Ph.D. degree from the Divinity School, University of Chicago in 1982, and has done additional study at the University of Heidelberg and the University of Tubingen in Germany.

He has been the recipient of the Fulbright-Hays Travel Grant, the Deutscher Akademischer Austauschdienst Language Grant and the Franklin Clark Fry Postdoctoral Fellowship. His books include, *Welcoming the Stranger: A Public Theology of Worship and Evangelism* (1992), *Worship and Evangelism: A Pastoral Handbook* (1990), *People Together,* a set of small group ministry manuals (1994), *Talking About Our Faith* (1998), *The Small Church Small Group Guide* (1998), *But Is It All True?* (2006), and *Testing The Spirits* (2006). *He has also contributed to A Story Worth Sharing: Engaging Evangelism* (2004), *The Ending of Mark and the Ends of God: Essays in Memory of Donald Harrisville Juel* (2005), and *To Teach, To Delight, and to Move: Theological Education in a Post-Christian World* (2006).

CONTACT INFORMATION:

E-mail: pkeifert@churchinnovations.org

**Church
Innovations**

1563 Como Avenue # 103
St Paul, Mn 55108
651-644-3653 ‖ 888-223-7631
www.churchinnovations.org

Is your congregation ready to move from
doing *mission to being* **missional?**

Then we invite you into a partnership... the
Partnership for Missional Church — a
journey of spiritual discernment that
empowers churches likd yours worldwide
to respond to God's mission, so that your
outreach and your life together as a church
are witnesses to Jesus Christ.

**Church
Innovations**

1563 Como Avenue # 103
St Paul, Mn 55108
651-644-3653 ‖ 888-223-7631
www.churchinnovations.org

PATRICK KEIFERT,
*President and founder of Church
Innovations, and has assembled a
team of Christ-centered consultants
who come alongside congregations
to nurture healthy change and
growth. Our consultants, with mini-
sterial and seminary experience, are
thought leaders in today's Church.*

*Since 1990, Church Innovations
research staff has combined both
quantitative methods and applied
ethnography (deep listening) to
help congregations discern what
God is doing in their communities.
This depth of experience has led
to refined processes and tools that
will support congregations as they
seek God's mission for them.*

Church FutureFinder – a guided self study of local church and community to aid in discerning the future of your church, especially its missional calling

 Congregational Discovery – deep listening by members of the congregation to their fellow members, gathering stories and descriptions of the church's culture in order to prepare to embrace God's missional vocation for them.

 Staff Covenanting - A prayerful, God-centered process that affirms and leverages staff gifts, helping to align them with the congregational vision.

 Growing Healthier Congregations – A process that sets forth habits for faith-based conversations that move congregations from fear and avoidance to discernment, decision, and action.

 Robust Church Development – Designed to inspire and equip congregations to embrace their missional challenges and respond to God's direction.

Conflict in Mission – a learning experience for judicatory staff members who want better ways of attending to full-blown conflict and also for helping churches learn habits that help them see oncoming conflict as potential energy for mission.

CHURCH INNOVATIONS ALWAYS WELCOMES YOUR SUPPORT IN PRAYER AND IN FINANCIAL CONTRIBUTIONS. PLEASE CONTACT US FOR SPECIFIC WAYS YOUR GIFTS WILL MAKE A DIFFERENCE IN OUR WORK.

OTHER BOOKS BY PATRICK KEIFERT

*Welcoming the Stranger: A Public Theology
of Worship and Evangelism (1992)*

*Worship and Evangelism:
A Pastoral Handbook (1990)*

*People Together, a set of small group
ministry manuals (1994)*

Talking About Our Faith (1998)

The Small Church Small Group Guide (1998)

But Is It All True? (2006),

Testing The Spirits (2006)

HE HAS ALSO CONTRIBUTED TO:

A Story Worth Sharing: Engaging Evangelism (2004)

*The Ending of Mark and the Ends of God:
Essays in Memory of Donald Harrisville Juel* (2005)

*To Teach, To Delight, and to Move: Theological Education
in a Post-Christian World* (2006)